MYSTERIES, LEGENDS, AND UNEXPLAINED PHENOMENA

DREAMS AND ASTRAL TRAVEL

MYSTERIES, LEGENDS, AND UNEXPLAINED PHENOMENA

Astrology and Divination

Bigfoot, Yeti, and Other Ape-Men

Dreams and Astral Travel

ESP, Psychokinesis, and Psychics

Fairies

Ghosts and Haunted Places

Lake and Sea Monsters

Magic and Alchemy

Mythical Creatures

Shamanism

Spirit Communications

UFOs and Aliens

Vampires

Werewolves

Witches and Wiccans

MYSTERIES, LEGENDS, AND UNEXPLAINED PHENOMENA

DREAMS AND ASTRAL TRAVEL

ROSEMARY ELLEN GUILEY

Consulting Editor: Rosemary Ellen Guiley

CHELSEA HOUSE
PUBLISHERS
An imprint of Infobase Publishing

DREAMS AND ASTRAL TRAVEL

Chelsea House
An imprint of Infobase Publishing
132 West 31st Street
New York NY 10001

Library of Congress Cataloging-in-Publication Data

Guiley, Rosemary.
  Dreams and astral travel / Rosemary Ellen Guiley.
    p. cm. — (Mysteries, legends, and unexplained phenomena)
  Includes bibliographical references and index.
  ISBN-13: 978-0-7910-9387-0 (hardcover : alk. paper)
    ISBN-10: 0-7910-9387-5 (hardcover : alk. paper) 1. Dreams. 2. Astral projection.
  I. Title. II. Series.

  BF1078.G847 2009
  133.9'5—dc22

                    2009014177

Text design by James Scotto-Lavino
Cover design by Ben Peterson

Printed in the United States of America

Bang EJB 10 9 8 7 6 5 4 3 2 1

This book is printed on acid-free paper.

Contents

Foreword

Did you ever have an experience that turned your whole world upside down? Maybe you saw a ghost or a UFO. Perhaps you had an unusual, vivid dream that seemed real. Maybe you suddenly knew that a certain event was going to happen in the future. Or, perhaps you saw a creature or a being that did not fit the description of anything known in the natural world. At first you might have thought your imagination was playing tricks on you. Then, perhaps, you wondered about what you experienced and went looking for an explanation.

Every day and night people have experiences they can't explain. For many people these events are life changing. Their comfort zone of what they can accept as "real" is put to the test. It takes only one such experience for people to question the reality of the mysterious worlds that might exist beyond the one we live in. Perhaps you haven't encountered the unknown, but you have an intense curiosity about it. Either way, by picking up this book, you've started an adventure to explore and learn more, and you've come to the right place! The book you hold has been written by a leading expert in the paranormal—someone who understands unusual experiences and who knows the answers to your questions.

As a seeker of knowledge, you have plenty of company. Mythology, folklore, and records of the past show that human beings have had paranormal experiences throughout history. Even prehistoric cave paintings and gravesites indicate that early humans had concepts of the supernatural and of an afterlife. Humans have always sought to understand paranormal experiences and to put them into a frame of reference that makes sense to us in our daily lives. Some of the greatest minds in history have grappled with questions about the paranormal. For example, Greek philosopher Plato pondered the nature of dreams and how we "travel" during them. Isaac Newton was interested in the esoteric study of alchemy, which has magical elements, and St. Thomas Aquinas explored the nature of angels and spirits. Philosopher William James joined organizations dedicated to psychical research; and even the inventor of the light bulb, Thomas Alva Edison, wanted to build a device that could talk to the dead. More recently, physicists such as David Bohm, Stephen Hawking, William Tiller, and Michio Kaku have developed ideas that may help explain how and why paranormal phenomena happen, and neuroscience researchers like Michael Persinger have explored the nature of consciousness.

Exactly what is a paranormal experience or phenomenon? "Para" is derived from a Latin term for "beyond." So "paranormal" means "beyond normal," or things that do not fit what we experience through our five senses alone and which do not follow the laws we observe in nature and in science. Paranormal experiences and phenomena run the gamut from the awesome and marvelous, such as angels and miracles, to the downright terrifying, such as vampires and werewolves.

Paranormal experiences have been consistent throughout the ages, but explanations of them have changed as societies, cultures, and technologies have changed. For example, our ancestors were much closer to the invisible realms. In times when life was simpler, they saw, felt, and experienced other realities on a daily basis. When night fell, the darkness was thick and quiet, and it was easier to see unusual things, such as ghosts. They had no electricity to keep the night lit up. They had no media for constant communication and entertainment. Travel was difficult. They had more time to notice subtle things that were just beyond their ordinary senses. Few doubted their experiences. They accepted the invisible realms as an extension of ordinary life.

Today, we have many distractions. We are constantly busy, from the time we wake up until we go to bed. The world is full of light and noise 24 hours a day, seven days a week. We have television, the Internet, computer games, and cell phones to keep us busy, busy, busy.

We are ruled by technology and science. Yet, we still have paranormal experiences very similar to those of our ancestors. Because these occurrences do not fit neatly into science and technology, many people think they are illusions, and there are plenty of skeptics always ready to debunk the paranormal and reinforce that idea.

In roughly the past 100 years, though, some scientists have studied the paranormal and attempted to find scientific evidence for it. Psychic phenomena have proven difficult to observe and measure according to scientific standards. However, lack of scientific proof does not mean paranormal experiences do not happen. Courageous scientists are still looking for bridges between science and the supernatural.

My personal experiences are behind my lifelong study of the paranormal. Like many children I had invisible playmates when I was very young, and I saw strange lights in the yard and woods that I instinctively knew were the nature spirits who lived there. Children seem to be very open to paranormal phenomena, but their ability to have these experiences often fades away as they become more involved in the outside world, or, perhaps, as adults tell them not to believe in what they experience, that it's only in their imagination. Even when I was very young, I was puzzled that other people would tell me with great authority that I did not experience what I knew I did.

A major reason for my interest in the paranormal is precognitive dreaming experienced by members of my family. Precognition means "fore knowing," or knowing the future. My mother had a lot of psychic experiences, including dreams of future events. As a teen it seemed amazing to me that dreams could show us the future. I was determined to learn more about this and to have such dreams myself. I found books that explained extrasensory perception, the knowing of information beyond the five senses. I learned about dreams and experimented with them. I taught myself to visit distant places in my dreams and to notice details about them that I could later verify in the physical world. I learned how to send people telepathic messages in dreams and how to receive messages in dreams. Every night became an exciting adventure.

Those interests led me to other areas of the paranormal. Pretty soon I was engrossed in studying all kinds of topics. I learned different techniques for divination, including the Tarot. I learned how to meditate. I took courses to develop my own psychic skills, and I gave psychic readings to others. Everyone has at least some natural psychic ability and can improve it with attention and practice.

Next I turned my attention to the skies, to ufology, and what might be "out there" in space. I studied the lore of angels and fairies. I delved into the dark shadowy realm of demons and monsters. I learned the principles of real magic and spell casting. I undertook investigations of haunted places. I learned how to see auras and do energy healing. I even participated in some formal scientific laboratory experiments for telepathy.

My studies led me to have many kinds of experiences that have enriched my understanding of the paranormal. I cannot say that I can prove anything in scientific terms. It may be some time yet before science and the paranormal stop flirting with each other and really get together. Meanwhile, we can still learn a great deal from our personal experiences. At the very least, our paranormal experiences contribute to our inner wisdom. I encourage others to do the same as I do. Look first for natural explanations of strange phenomena. If natural explanations cannot be found or seem unlikely, consider paranormal explanations. Many paranormal experiences fall into a vague area, where although natural causes might exist, we simply don't know what could explain them. In that case I tell people to trust their intuition that they had a paranormal experience. Sometimes the explanation makes itself known later on.

I have concluded from my studies and experiences that invisible dimensions are layered upon our world, and that many paranormal experiences occur when there are openings between worlds. The doorways often open at unexpected times. You take a trip, visit a haunted place, or have a strange dream—and suddenly reality shifts. You get a glimpse behind the curtain that separates the ordinary from the extraordinary.

The books in this series will introduce you to these exciting and mysterious subjects. You'll learn many things that will astonish you. You'll be given lots of tips for how to explore the paranormal on your own. Paranormal investigation is a popular field, and you don't have to be a scientist or a full-time researcher to explore it. There are many things you can do in your free time. The knowledge you gain from these books will help prepare you for any unusual and unexpected experiences.

As you go deeper into your study of the paranormal, you may come up with new ideas for explanations. That's one of the appealing aspects of paranormal investigation—there is always room for bold ideas. So, keep an open and curious mind, and think big. Mysterious worlds are waiting for you!

—Rosemary Ellen Guiley

Introduction

As long as human beings have dreamed, they have wondered about the purpose and meaning of the images that pass through their minds in sleep. Are dreams nonsense, or are they meaningful? People decided in ancient times that dreams do have meaning and are so important that kings and heads of state should pay attention to them.

Over the course of history the significance of dreams has risen and fallen and risen several times. Today we value dreams, considering them an important part of our well-being and a way to understand what goes on inside of us. Dreams also are held by many to have deep, spiritual importance as a way for us to participate in the cosmic scheme of things.

Dreams are worth exploring and understanding. There are many approaches to do so available today, and each person may find the one that feels most comfortable and makes the most sense. One of the fundamental concepts in working with dreams today is that only the dreamer can truly understand the meaning his or her own dreams. Others, such as dream experts and professional counselors, can help the process but cannot determine for someone else what their dreams mean. This is a significant change from ancient times, when professional dream interpreters or priests held all the power in deciphering dreams. Dreams now take on a deep personal meaning for individuals, who must interpret them for themselves.

Dreamwork is like learning a secret, coded language. Dreams speak in mysterious symbols and in odd dramas, but once you learn the key to decoding them, they reveal all kinds of hidden, inner treasures.

On the surface dreams often seem bizarre and senseless. Learning their language is easier than it might seem. In fact, anyone who follows the tips offered in this book will quickly be decoding their own dreams. Some dreams reveal their meanings right away and some require more time and work, but the rewards are great. Dreamwork is interesting and fun, and it is beneficial, too.

I have studied dreams most of my life. My interest in them began in my teens, when my mother started discussing some of her dreams with me. She had precognitive dreams, that is, she dreamed of things that were going to happen in the future. The idea that we can dream the future fascinated me. I wanted to know more about this strange landscape that unfolds when we sleep.

I read everything I could find on dreams and also on psychic experiences. I started experimenting with my own dreams. I found that I could know that I was dreaming while I was dreaming. I could "travel" to a distant place of my choice and come back with accurate descriptions of what I had seen. I could send and receive messages in dreams. I could look into the future.

My results varied quite a bit. Sometimes I was successful, sometimes only modestly successful, and sometimes not successful at all. Nonetheless, I was amazed and excited by my results.

My research into dreams took me into history, psychology, mythology, anthropology, parapsychology, science, and medicine. I learned what the ancients thought about dreams and how that compares to what we believe about dreams today. I studied the views of pioneer psychologists such as Sigmund Freud and Carl G. Jung. I examined the dream beliefs and practices of other cultures. I read about the research and experiments of scientists to understand the mechanisms of dreaming, and the experiments of parapsychologists, who are interested in the psychic side of dreams. I also looked into the role of dreams in healing.

Finally, I explored how dreams can be used as sources of creativity, invention, and inspiration. Some of humanity's greatest advancements have come from dreams.

While the big picture of dreams is exciting, dreams are probably most important on a personal level. They help us sort through our feelings, understand ourselves, and find solutions to problems. Paying attention to your dreams on a regular basis is rewarding. I have kept a dream journal for most of my life and have recorded hundreds and hundreds of my own dreams. Dreamwork has helped me get through difficult times, has aided the creativity of my writing, and has helped me see patterns in how I deal with situations in life.

This book will introduce you to the major aspects of dreams, dreaming, and dreamwork. The literature on dreams is vast. I have several hundred books on the subject in my library. In this book, you'll get the highlights on all the important aspects of dreams, as well as some tips for doing your own dream interpretation and exploration.

The first several chapters lay a foundation. Chapter 1, "A Gift from the Gods," looks at the role of dreams in the ancient world, the heritage on which we base our present beliefs about dreams. Chapter 2, "The Fall and Rebirth of Dreams," traces how changing attitudes toward dreams influenced whether or not people paid attention to them. Attitudes toward dreams are wrapped up closely in religious and spiritual beliefs. I have kept to an emphasis on Western history due to the limits of space.

Chapter 3, "Science Ventures into Dreamland," covers what we have learned about the process of dreaming, such as what goes on in the brain and body when we enter the dreamscape.

Chapter 4, "The Virtual Reality of Lucid Dreaming," begins exploring the mysterious, psychic, creative, and healing aspects of dreaming. In lucid dreams, the dreamer knows he or she is having a dream while it is underway and sometimes can control it. Chapter 5, "Night Flying," launches into the astral travel side of dreaming. Chapter 6, "The Astral World," explores the landscape of dreaming described by lucid and astral traveling dreamers.

Chapter 7, "The Psychic Side of Dreams," looks at how people dream of the future and scientific studies of dream telepathy. Those psychic factors lead to Chapter 8, "Dreams That Heal," which describes accounts of how people are healed in dreams or are given valuable information about their health.

Chapter 9, "Understanding Your Dreams," offers guidelines for how to interpret dreams. Then Chapter 10, "Dream It, Do It," looks at how dreams deliver breakthrough ideas. This will also provide tips for asking one's dreams for ideas that are needed in waking life.

Readers might have family members or friends who are also interested in dreams and in talking about them. Sharing dreams increases their benefits. There are also many groups and organizations devoted to dreams, where one can find like-minded people. Some people also do dreamwork with professional counselors from time to time. There are times when it is useful or best to have professional guidance.

Those who start working with their dreams may stay with it for much of their life, the same as one might with an exercise program that is good for physical health. Sometimes your dreams have a lot to say, and sometimes they fall into the background. One's dreams respond to one's needs, and for those who develop good dream habits, they will serve well.

1

A Gift from the Gods

Around 1400 BCE—about 3,400 years ago—a young Egyptian prince named Thutmose goes hunting one day in the hot desert on the Giza Plateau. Thutmose is the son of the pharaoh Amenhotep II, and his name means "Born of the God Thoth." He admires three majestic and mysterious pyramids that tower over the sand and the even more mysterious Sphinx nearby. The rule of the pharaohs is in its 18th Dynasty, but these structures are older still, their origins lost to time. Neither the prince nor any of his royal advisors know who built these massive structures or why. The full form of the Sphinx is unknown, for only its massive head juts out of the sand. It has been in the desert for a very long time.

The prince harbors great ambitions to rule Egypt. He is not the first-born son of the pharaoh, however, which means his older brother will inherit the throne when their father dies.

Thutmose rests in the shadow of the Sphinx's head, falls asleep, and dreams. In his dream the sun god, who is embodied by the Sphinx, named Horemakhet-Khepri-Ra-Atum, comes to him and complains that his body is covered by sand. The god tells Thutmose that if he will clear away the sand so that the limbs and health of the Sphinx can be restored, he will be rewarded with the kingship of Egypt.

When the prince awakens, he is excited. He does as the dream instructs. In 1419 BCE, after casting his older brother out of power, he becomes pharaoh, the eighth ruler of the 18th Dynasty. He becomes

Thutmose IV, and takes the throne name of Men-kheperu-re, meaning "Everlasting are the Manifestations of Re."

In gratitude of the dream, Thutmose IV records the story of his dream in hieroglyphics on a stele—a carved slab of limestone—and plants it between the uncovered lion paws of the Sphinx.

Some historians dispute this story, arguing that Thutmose grabbed power and then made up a dream to justify his actions. No one could fault him if the gods had directed him to a certain course of action.

Either way, the stele, which still exists today, is a testimony to the power of dreams in changing the course of history.

Dreaming may seem an ordinary part of life today, but in ancient times dreams were considered gifts of the gods. They revealed the future, were important in healing, and were used magically to influence the thoughts and actions of others. People did not "have" dreams; they were "given" or "sent" dreams. Good dreams were sent by gods and bad dreams, which were believed to cause illness, were sent by demons.

The Western tradition of beliefs about dreams and their meanings dates to the Sumerians, Assyrians, Babylonians, and Egyptians. Professional dream interpreters studied dreams for information of state and political importance and for solutions to community disputes and problems. People practiced dream **incubation**. That is the practice of instructing dreams to answer specific questions or to become avenues of healing.

The oldest dream book in existence comes from Assyria. The Assyrian Dream Book is actually a collection of clay cylinders. They were found at Nineveh in the library of the famous Assyrian king Ashurbanipal, who ruled from 669–626 BCE. The cylinders show that Assyrian dream interpretation relied heavily upon contraries, or opposites. For example, to dream of being blessed by a god actually meant one would be punished by a god.

DREAMS IN EGYPT

The Egyptians absorbed some of the Assyrian and Mesopotamian dream practices into their own culture. They considered dreams to be a "revelation of truth." If a person was given instructions in a dream, he had to follow them or else he would suffer misfortune. If dreams were not interpreted properly, the gods would be angry.

In Egypt the guardians of dream interpretation were called lector priests, or "Masters of the Secret Things" and "Scribes of the Double House of Life." The priests were learned men who kept the sacred books containing the religious lore and laws and magical rites. They worked in libraries that were part of many temples throughout the land. People consulted them for dream interpretation and spells to solve problems. The temple books of dreams and magic were carefully guarded in order to protect the status of the priests. The lector priests were forerunners of today's psychotherapists. They consulted with people about the meanings of their dreams and offered other advice.

In interpreting dreams the Egyptians also relied heavily upon contraries, or meanings that were the opposite of the contents of a dream. They also relied upon puns and plays on words, which are techniques that still work today.

Dreams were an important part of magical practices. The lector priests had many spells and rituals for "sending" messages into the dreaming sleep of another person to try to influence their thinking and actions. Even the dead could send dreams to the living.

The dead played an important role in Egyptian dream magic. Since the dead lived in another realm, they were believed to have great power, which could be controlled through magic. The dead were summoned to enforce curses and spells via dreams and also to appear in dreams in order to answer questions about the future. People who had drowned in the Nile were especially believed to have a divine gift of prophecy and were commanded to come to the dreams of a priest or magician.

Figure 1.1 *This life-size statue of a chief lector priest was discovered by archeologists in 1860. In ancient Egypt, lector priests watched over the sacred texts in dream temples, interpreted people's dreams, and cast spells to solve problems.* (Roger Wood/Corbis)

DREAMS AMONG THE EARLY HEBREWS

The early Hebrews placed a high value on dreams as real experiences of the direct voice of God. The Old Testament, or Torah, contains many examples of dreams and waking visions as primary ways that a concerned God speaks to human beings. Sometimes the descriptions do not distinguish clearly between a dream and a waking vision. Perhaps the difference was not important then. Professional dream interpreters were highly respected by the Hebrews.

The first biblical reference to a dream is in Genesis 15:12-16. While the prophet Abram (later renamed Abraham) was in a deep dreaming sleep, God gave him the prophecy that Abram's descendants would be enslaved in a foreign land (Egypt) for 400 years, after which they would be liberated with great possessions and returned to their own land.

Abraham's grandson, Jacob, had significant dreams, the most famous of which is recorded in Genesis 28:11-22. Jacob had a dream of a ladder to heaven filled with angels moving up and down it. He was so awestruck by the dream that he called the place where he slept "the house of God . . . the gate of heaven."

Jacob's son Joseph, who was sold into slavery in Egypt by his brothers, excelled in dream interpretation, and thus he gained the pharaoh's favor.

Many other great biblical prophets, patriarchs, and rulers were inspired and directed by dreams or visions, among them Moses, Samuel, Saul, Solomon, Elijah, Jeremiah, Job, Isaiah, Ezekiel, and Daniel. Losing contact with God through dreams was a crisis, a serious loss of power.

By about the eighth century BCE, the Hebrew prophets became concerned about false prophets using false dreams to sway people. The common people were told to beware of false prophets dealing in dreams. Dream incubation was not encouraged but was practiced.

In the sixteenth century CE an important Jewish text on dream interpretation was published; it moved dreams away from divine prophecy and more into ordinary life. The text was first titled *Chelmin* ("Dream Mediator") and then retitled *Pitron Chalomot* ("Interpretation of Dreams"). The author, philosopher and rabbi Solomon Almoli, said that most dreams represent the dreamer's own thoughts and concerns.

Dreams come from a person's own imagination, he said, woven by an inner "Spinner of Dreams." Almoli believed that the emotions in a dream were important to the interpretation, because they revealed

Did Dream Magic Birth a Hero?

Alexander the Great (356–323 BCE) was one of the greatest conquering heroes of the classical world. He spread the Greek empire far and wide around the Mediterranean. He seemed unstoppable. How did he do it? According to legend, Alexander was half-god, half-human, and his birth was arranged by dream magic.

The ancient Egyptians were masters of magic. They knew how to cause people to have certain dreams that would influence events and perhaps even the course of history.

The story goes that Nectanebo, the last native king of Egypt, used dream magic on Alexander's mother, the Greek queen Olympias, and her husband, King Philip of Macedon. First Nectanebo caused Olympias to dream that the Egyptian god Amun would make love to her, and she would bear a god. Nectanebo accomplished this through sympathetic magic. He poured the extracted juices of certain desert plants over a wax doll representing the queen while he recited a spell. Nectanebo then turned his attention to Philip of Macedon. He said a spell over a hawk, which flew to the sleeping Philip and told him to dream that Olympias was going to bear a child who was the son of a god.

The magic was successful, and Olympias became pregnant. When Alexander was born, his divine origin was unquestioned. He was believed to be half Greek and half Egyptian god.

Alexander was probably only a mortal who possessed great abilities and charisma. But in those times rulers and heroes were given divine pedigrees to enhance their status. Nonetheless, dream magic was indeed practiced, and people believed that gods could be made through dreams.

true emotions below the surface, "nothing other than the thoughts of [the dreamer's] heart."[1] These ideas are part of the foundation of dreamwork today.

DREAMS IN GREECE AND ROME

The ancient Greeks continued many of the dream beliefs and practices of the Egyptians, Mesopotamians, and Hebrews. According to Homer, dreams were events that were witnessed: The Greeks did not "have" dreams but "saw" them.[2] In the earliest beliefs, the gods made real visits to the dreamer, entering a bedroom through the keyhole and standing at the head of the bed while they delivered their message.

Like the Hebrews, the Greeks made little or no distinction between dreams and visions. Around the seventh century BCE, a shamanic and Eastern idea about dreams was introduced to Greek culture: rather than being visited by gods, the dreamer traveled out-of-body at night to meet the gods.

The great Greek philosophers paid a lot of attention to dreams. Plato (427?–347 BCE) believed that dreams could be controlled in order to see truth. Control came from leading a righteous life.

Aristotle (384–322 BCE), one of Plato's pupils, took a radical departure from the conventional dream wisdom of the times. He said most dreams are entirely natural and are the result of ordinary experiences.[3] The gods would not waste themselves on sending dreams to ordinary mortals. Nor would the gods waste dreams on animals. It was obvious that animals dreamed because of the way they twitch and moan during sleep, Aristotle said.

Aristotle's views about dreams were not popular during his day, but they did influence Roman thinkers and, many centuries later, important Christian theologians and philosophers.

The Roman philosopher Cicero (106 BCE–43 BCE) said that if the gods truly wanted to warn people of impending events, they should do so during the day and under clear circumstances, not during the confusion of dreams at night.

On the opposite side, Augustus Caesar (63 BCE–14 CE) took dreams so seriously that he proclaimed a new law: anyone who dreamed about the Roman commonwealth was required to proclaim the dream in the marketplace.

Plutarch (46?–c.120) argued that everybody—not only priests—could experience prophecy in dreams.

As Christianity struggled to gain a foothold after the death of Jesus, it survived on a merger of Greek, Roman, and Hebrew cultures. But as Christianity grew, dreams declined in importance.

DREAMS IN EARLY CHRISTIANITY

Initially, Christianity continued honoring dreams and visions as a primary way that God communicated with humans. Dreams and visions literally shaped the birthing and early development of Christianity. Angels, the communicators of God, appeared to people in dreams in ways similar to the dream appearances of the gods of the Greeks.

The births of John the Baptist and Jesus were forecast in dreams or visionary experiences. After the birth of Jesus his father, Joseph, was warned in a dream to flee to Egypt to avoid King Herod's campaign to kill male infants who might threaten his rule. Jesus had numerous visionary experiences during his life that might have taken place in dreams or dreamlike states. For example, Jesus has an important confrontation with the devil after he has fasted for 40 days and nights in the wilderness. Such a lengthy period of physical deprivation could significantly affect dreaming and alter consciousness into dreamlike states. Matthew 4:1-11 and Luke 4:1-12 tell how the devil tempted Jesus three times. First the devil tried to persuade Jesus to perform miracles to prove he is the Son of God. Then he offered Jesus all the kingdoms of the world in exchange for worship. Jesus resisted and banished the devil.

After the arrest of Jesus, Pontius Pilate's wife was warned in a dream that her husband should have nothing to do with him. Following the crucifixion of Jesus, the apostles had many dreams and visionary experiences that aided them in their mission to spread the Gospel. One famous account concerns St. Peter, who was imprisoned by Herod Agrippa, who planned to execute him. The night before he was to be condemned, Peter slept in his cell bound in chains and guarded by two soldiers. An angel awakened him, freed him of his chains, and led him out of the prison. Peter at first thought he was dreaming, then believed he had a real visitation. The experience may actually have been a combination of dreaming and visionary experience.

Many of the early church fathers who shaped the beliefs of the new religion were Platonic philosophers and Greek converts. They believed in the tradition of God speaking through dreams and visions. But a major turn in the opposite direction took place in the fourth century, and it centered on one man: Jerome, who is discussed in Chapter 2.

2

The Fall and Rebirth of Dreams

In the fourth century Jerome is a bright young man raised in an affluent Christian family. He is drawn to pagan beliefs and devotes himself to an intense study of Greek and Roman classics. Then he has an experience that affects Western beliefs about dreams for the next 1,600 years. During a severe illness, he has a dream that changes the course of his life. He is taken before God and a tribunal and is accused of being a pagan despite his claims of being a Christian:

> Suddenly I was caught up in the spirit and dragged before the judgment seat of the Judge; and here the light was so bright, and those who stood around were so radiant, that I cast myself upon the ground and did not dare to look up. Asked who and what I was I replied: "I am a Christian." But He who presided said: "Thou liest, thou art a follower of Cicero and not of Christ. For 'where thy treasure is, there will thy heart be also.'" Instantly I became dumb, and amid the strokes of the lash—for He had ordered me to be scourged—I was tortured more severely still by the fire of conscience, considering with myself that verse, "In the grave who shall give thee thanks?" Yet for all that I began to cry and to bewail myself, saying: "Have mercy upon me, O Lord: have mercy upon me." Amid the sound of the scourges this

cry still made itself heard. At last the bystanders, falling down before the knees of Him who presided, prayed
that He would have pity on my youth, and that He would
give me space to repent of my error. He might still, they
urged, inflict torture on me, should I ever again read the
works of the Gentiles. . . .

Accordingly I made an oath and called upon His name,
saying "Lord, if ever again I possess worldly books, or if
ever again I read such, I have denied Thee." Dismissed,
then, on taking this oath, I returned to the upper world,
and, to the surprise of all, I opened upon them eyes so
drenched with tears that my distress served to convince
even the credulous. And that this was no sleep nor idle
dream, such as those by which we are often mocked, I
call to witness the tribunal before which I lay, and the
terrible judgment which I feared. . . . I profess that my
shoulders were black and blue, that I felt the bruises long
after I awoke from my sleep, and that thenceforth I read
the books of God with a zeal greater than I had previ-
ously given to the books of men.[1]

Shaken, Jerome retires to the desert as a hermit for several years.
He then resumes his career as scholar and biblical consultant and heads
a monastic community in Bethlehem.

Despite his own dream experience, Jerome denies the importance
of dreams. He acknowledges that dreams can reveal divine things, but
he also feels that the impure and unrighteous can twist dreams for
their own self-serving ends. He declares that the word of God cannot
be sought through pagan practices of dream incubation.

Jerome makes his greatest contribution to Christianity by trans-
lating the Bible from Greek and Hebrew into the Latin Vulgate. He
chooses negative words to describe dreams, associating them with
witchcraft and fortune-telling.[2] Jerome's translation remains the au-
thoritative version in Western Christianity into modern times.

DREAMS IN DECLINE

As Christianity spread throughout Europe and the classical world, dreams went further into decline. The great pagan dream temples were converted to Christian churches or were shut.

In the thirteenth century St. Thomas Aquinas, one of the greatest scholars of the Christian church, added to the decline of the dream by supporting the Aristotlean view that knowledge of the world must come only through the senses and rational thought. Aquinas wanted to modernize the church, and he felt Aristotle's philosophy would do so. Aquinas said that dreams have no significance because people have no direct contact with spiritual reality.

Because of biblical tradition Aquinas had to acknowledge that some dreams could come from God. But for the most part, he said, dreams come from demons, false opinions, and natural causes such as conditions of the body. It was not unlawful to divine from dreams as long as one was certain that the dreams were from a divine source and not from demons.

Dreams fell by the wayside as a direct communication with God. The Reformation of the sixteenth century brought the end of widespread belief in miracles and supernatural events, including dream visions. By the eighteenth century the dream was nearly finished as a spiritual experience. At the popular level dream interpretation was sought from wizards and astrologers.

Influential philosophers also contributed to the spiritual demise of the dream. For example, René Descartes (who made the famous statement, "I think, therefore I am") supported the Aristotlean view. He was convinced that dreams resulted from food eaten prior to sleep. Oddly, one of his most important philosophical works, *Discourse on the Method* (1637), was inspired by a dream.

THE RETURN OF DREAMS

In the late nineteenth century psychical research developed as a scientific approach to studying the paranormal. Important to that research

Figure 2.1 *French philosopher René Descartes works at his desk. Descartes believed that dreams were essentially meaningless, but his famous* Discourse on the Method *(1637) was inspired by a dream.* (Time & Life Pictures/Getty Images)

were dreams, for many precognitive, telepathic, and extraordinary experiences were reported to take place in dreams. The founders of the Society for Psychical Research (SPR) in London collected cases of telepathy and precognition in dreams.

Later studies of extrasensory perception (ESP) experiences in general, such as those done in the 1960s by American parapsychologist Louisa Rhine, showed that dreams are involved in 33 to 68 percent of all cases. Dreams account for 25 percent of all cases of telepathy and approximately 60 to 70 percent of all cases of precognition. About 10 percent of ESP experiences occur when an individual is at the border of sleep.[3]

Dreams also regained importance at the turn of the twentieth century in the new field of psychology, pioneered by Sigmund Freud. In his book *The Interpretation of Dreams* (1900), Freud called dreams the "royal road" to the unconscious. He said they are wish fulfillments of repressed infantile desires.[4] Events during the day, or "day residues," commonly appear in dreams. If a dream doesn't disguise anything, then it is a mere fantasy, Freud said. Although Freud acknowledged that sleep was conducive to telepathy, he said dreams have little practical importance.

Freud's pupil Carl G. Jung disagreed. He centered his branch of psychology on dreams. Jung had a rich dream life, full of symbols that he called **archetypes**, that is, symbols having a meaning beyond their significance to the individual. Archetypal symbols come from a pool of human experience shared by all people throughout history. They appear in myth, legend, and folk tales. Jung believed archetypes are endless, created by the repetition of situations and experiences engraved upon collective human experience. God, birth, death, rebirth, power, magic, the sun, the moon, the wind, animals, and the elements are examples of archetypes. Archetypes, according to Jung, are psychic forces that demand to be taken seriously, and dreams contain both personal symbols and archetypal symbols.[5]

Jung also said that the purpose of dreams is compensatory. That is, they provide information about the self that helps a person to maintain inner balance and harmony.

Jung disagreed so strongly with Freud over dreams that it was a major factor in the split of their professional relationship. Both men went on to develop branches of psychology that are used in counseling today.

Other theories adding to Freud's and Jung's work have been put forward on the nature, function, and meaning of dreams. However, psychotherapists upheld the ancient beliefs that dreamwork could only be done by qualified professionals; therapists had replaced the old dream priests of long ago.

Since about the 1970s dreamwork has become more democratic and less dependent upon professionals. Anyone can do it, and there are many books and other sources of help. Many people still prefer to work with professional therapists, or at least consult with them from time to time. Other people pursue their own dreamwork or join informal groups devoted to dreamwork.

Dreams are of interest to the scientific community. Scientists study the mechanics of dreaming in the brain, the diagnostic and healing content of dreams, the psychic content of dreams, and the nature of lucid dreams and shared dreams.

DREAMS AS EXCEPTIONAL HUMAN EXPERIENCES

Many of the dreams we experience are more than dreams; they are **exceptional human experiences** (EHE). The term "exceptional human experience" was coined in 1990 by researcher Rhea A. White to describe a wide range of non-ordinary and inexplicable experiences reported by people. Many of these experiences have a powerful impact upon people and can even change the course of their lives. An example of an exceptional human experience type of dream would be a miraculous healing that occurs during dreaming sleep. Other examples would be a vivid dream in which someone meets a religious figure, or has a conversation with someone who has died, or has a profound and accurate vision of the future.

THREE LEVELS TO DREAMS

Regardless of whether a dream is ordinary, reflecting daily life, or extraordinary, taking the dreamer into an otherworldly experience, it

The Dreamtime

The Aborigines of Australia, whose culture is about 65,000 years old, believe in a parallel dream reality to the waking world. It is called the "Dreamtime," a term coined in 1899 by anthropologists studying them. Some Aborigines prefer the term "The Dreaming."

The Dreamtime is an "Everywhen," existing everywhere and beyond time. It is the story of creation and myth and the values and laws of the cosmos. The Dreamtime is more real than waking reality. It holds the spiritual power of all things.

For the Aborigines the mythic age is not in the past but is still alive and parallel to the real world. At night a person's soul leaves this world and enters that realm. There is a continuing interaction between the two realms.

Some believe that at some time in humanity's early history, people may have existed wholly in a dreamlike state of consciousness such as the Dreamtime. Psychologist Julian Jaynes theorizes that humanity did not learn consciousness until around 3000 BCE. As people moved out of the dream state and more into waking consciousness, the dream state receded to the world of sleep, according to Jaynes. Nighttime dreams became a psychic and spiritual lifeline to the source of all being. Over the course of time, humankind pulled farther and farther away from knowing dreams as a living reality.

The Aborigines have retained that connection to the living reality of dreams.

Figure 2.2 *A crocodile and several fish can be seen in this Aboriginal "Dreamtime" painting.* (AAAC/Topham/The Image Works)

has multiple layers of meanings. Dreams are like onions: They have layer after layer of meanings. There are three main levels to dreams:

1 *Personal level.* Everything in a dream expresses a part of one's self and one's activities, thoughts, concerns, and emotions.

2 *Archetypal level.* Some elements in a dream express a "big" meaning beyond daily life. These images or symbols address the human journey through life.

3   *Transpersonal level.* Dreams are experiences of cosmic consciousness, in which the universe is revealed. The boundaries of time and space disappear. The dreamer sees the past and the future and realizes the ever-present now. He or she sees into other realms beyond the physical world and feels deeply connected to the divine and all things.

THE REWARDS OF DREAMWORK

Throughout history people have derived meaning and benefit from examining their dreams. Different aspects of dreams have been emphasized at different times in history, but the bottom line remains the same: No matter what the skeptics and critics have said, people believe that dreams are vitally important.

It's not necessary to study dreams for a long time before getting insight from them. Dreamwork is amazingly productive. The more it's done the more rewarding it becomes and the more one's understanding of dreams deepens. Reading about dream techniques and how others have interpreted their dreams can help one learn about their own dreams. Quite a bit of dreamwork can be done alone, but sometimes it is helpful to work with another person, such as a counselor or therapist, who is professionally trained.

Dreams are a source of energy and renewal. The high purpose of dreams is to help people find the meaning in life. All experiences, good and bad, have a purpose that contributes to the meaning of life and one's ability to enjoy it and prosper. Everyone has good and bad experiences throughout life. Dreams can help one to maximize the good and weather the bad.

Science Ventures into Dreamland

Scientific study of dreams began in earnest in 1953 when research-ers at the University of Chicago verified that a dream is likely to be in progress during **rapid eye movement** (REM). This phase of sleep is characterized by fluttering eyelids and other physiological symptoms, combined with particular brain-wave patterns.

What really is a dream? There is no definitive answer to this question. Science can explain a great deal about the mechanics of dreaming, but the exact substance of a dream and the reason why people have dreams remain a mystery. Some scientists believe that dreams are created only by the interplay of chemicals in the brain and have no psychological or spiritual value. Others believe that dreams are vital to the total health and the survival of a person and to the survival of humanity.

THE PHYSICAL PROCESS OF DREAMING

Dreaming originates in the brain stem and is controlled by neu-rotransmitters that turn dreams on and off. The "on switch" uses ace-tylcholine to begin the dream. The "off switch" uses norepinephrine and serotonin to end it. Norepinephrine and serotonin are necessary to imprint messages in long-term memory, which may explain why we forget the majority of our dreams. Since the two chemicals are suppressed during the dreaming process, dreams cannot be stored in long-term memory without help, such as writing them down or recording them upon awakening.

When the chemicals are suppressed, the acetylcholine allows electrical signals to be sent to the cortex. The brain stem neurons also start a theta rhythm in the hippocampus. This is a seahorse-shaped brain structure believed responsible for memory storage. Meanwhile, the nerves that usually carry information from the outside world shut down.

If the dream occurs during the REM phase of sleep, the sleeper experiences increased heart and respiration rates and a state of temporary paralysis. The brain stem freezes muscular activity to prevent the sleeper from acting out his or her dream.

TYPES OF DREAMS

Dreams differ significantly according to when in the sleep pattern they occur. There are four stages of non-REM (NREM) sleep that precede REM sleep.[1] As the sleeper descends through stages one through four, brain waves decrease in frequency. After reaching stage four, the sleeper reverses the process and ends up back in stage one. Then REM sleep begins, when the most vivid dreaming takes place. The stages are:

1   Light sleep, in which the brain shifts from the alpha waves of wakefulness to theta waves of sleepiness. It is easy to awaken someone in light sleep. Fragmentary dream images are common, including jumbled images, voices, and sensations of falling.

2   Deepening sleep, characterized by mostly theta waves. This stage usually lasts only a few minutes.

3   Deep sleep, in which the theta waves slow to delta.

4   Deep sleep, in which more than half of the brain wave activity is in delta, with the remainder in theta. It is difficult to awaken a person in deep sleep.

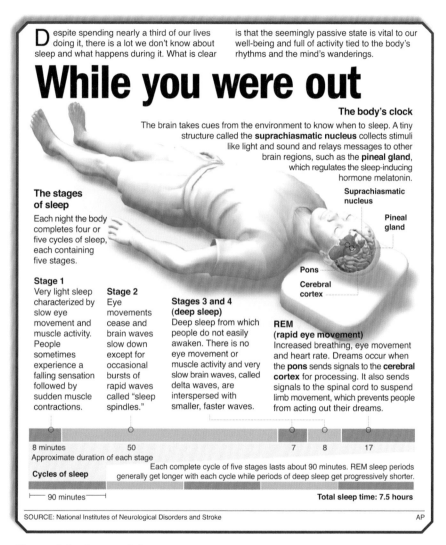

Despite spending nearly a third of our lives doing it, there is a lot we don't know about sleep and what happens during it. What is clear is that the seemingly passive state is vital to our well-being and full of activity tied to the body's rhythms and the mind's wanderings.

While you were out

The body's clock

The brain takes cues from the environment to know when to sleep. A tiny structure called the **suprachiasmatic nucleus** collects stimuli like light and sound and relays messages to other brain regions, such as the **pineal gland**, which regulates the sleep-inducing hormone melatonin.

The stages of sleep

Each night the body completes four or five cycles of sleep, each containing five stages.

Suprachiasmatic nucleus

Pineal gland

Pons

Cerebral cortex

Stage 1
Very light sleep characterized by slow eye movement and muscle activity. People sometimes experience a falling sensation followed by sudden muscle contractions.

Stage 2
Eye movements cease and brain waves slow down except for occasional bursts of rapid waves called "sleep spindles."

Stages 3 and 4 (deep sleep)
Deep sleep from which people do not easily awaken. There is no eye movement or muscle activity and very slow brain waves, called delta waves, are interspersed with smaller, faster waves.

REM (rapid eye movement)
Increased breathing, eye movement and heart rate. Dreams occur when the **pons** sends signals to the **cerebral cortex** for processing. It also sends signals to the spinal cord to suspend limb movement, which prevents people from acting out their dreams.

| 8 minutes | 50 | | 7 | 8 | 17 |

Approximate duration of each stage

Cycles of sleep

Each complete cycle of five stages lasts about 90 minutes. REM sleep periods generally get longer with each cycle while periods of deep sleep get progressively shorter.

├─ 90 minutes ─┤

Total sleep time: 7.5 hours

SOURCE: National Institutes of Neurological Disorders and Stroke

AP

Figure 3.1 *Stages of sleep.* (Associated Press)

These stages then reverse, and REM sleep begins.

All mammals (except the spiny anteater) and a few types of birds and reptiles experience REM sleep. In humans REM sleep decreases with age. Fetuses as young as 23 weeks spend nearly all their time in REM, and newborns spend about eight hours per day in REM. Up to 50 percent of the sleep of infants and small children is spent in REM. Adult sleep is 20 percent REM; for the elderly it is only 15 percent.

Four or five REM stages occur nightly, at about 90-minute intervals. The length of each session increases as the night goes on, until the average adult has spent about two hours in REM by morning.

People awakened during REM sleep are highly likely to remember their dreams, which differ from NREM dreams in their vividness, complexity, and generally bizarre nature. External factors such as noises can be immediately incorporated into REM dreams. For example, the sound of a car door slamming outside may become an explosion in a dream.

Non-REM dreams are more logical and concern current or recent events in the dreamer's life. These are the "day residues" defined by Sigmund Freud.

Hypnagogic dreams occur as we fall asleep, in the gray "twilight" between consciousness and sleep. Hypnagogic dreams are characterized by jumbled words and images, especially faces. Similar dreams are experienced in the **hypnapompic state**, which is the "twilight" that occurs in the transition from sleep to wakefulness.

WHY PEOPLE DREAM

The ancients were certain that the purpose of dreams was to learn the future, receive guidance, and heal the body.

Most scientists agree that dreaming—at least REM dreaming—plays a part in the learning process. Theta waves are active in the hippocampus during REM, and the hippocampus is involved in memory processing. In humans the hippocampus doesn't become functional until the age of two, the earliest age that most people can remember their dreams.

Some psychologists believe dreams to be compensatory and healing; they help people process and balance their emotions. Individuals

Figure 3.2 *Hypnagogic images are abstract shapes that present themselves on the threshold of sleep.* (Mary Evans Picture Library/The Image Works)

see personal and spiritual benefit to dreaming, with help for solving problems, getting ideas, and providing help in major life transitions.

Clinical psychologist and dream researcher Montague Ullman advanced the hypothesis that our dreams are not concerned primarily with people as individuals, but rather with the survival of the human species. Granted, individuals are the stars of their nightly shows, but looking beyond the personal meanings of dreams, it can be seen that they do address a larger social arena. Dreams reveal to people their state of connectedness to the whole of humanity, and how they feel about it, according to Ullman.[2]

The human species has been so fragmented into different cultures and geographies that the survival of the whole is at risk, said Ullman. Dreaming holds humanity together.

In quantum physics the model of David Bohm's implicate order supports this hypothesis of dreams as necessary for survival of the

Quick Dream FAQs

Got questions about dreams? Following are answers to the most common things people want to know.

Do people dream every night?
Scientific research indicates that, with few exceptions, everyone dreams every night. A small number of people who have suffered brain damage experience a loss of dreaming. How people cope depends on the extent of brain damage and its effects on the nervous system and senses. Some people experience difficulty sleeping.

Why are dreams sometimes hard to remember?
Stress, food, and medication can affect sleep patterns and in turn affect recall ability. Also, natural chemicals in the brain that are related to memory decrease during sleep.

Does everyone dream in color?
About 75 percent of people dream in color. More women dream in color than men. It's not unusual to dream primarily in color and also occasionally have black-and-white dreams.

How long do dreams last?
Most dreams are very short, ranging from a half-minute or so to several minutes in length. Some dreams can run as long as 15 to 20 minutes.

Do men and women dream differently?
Women's dreams contain more dialogue, social interaction, emotion, and detail. Men's dreams contain more action and male figures, and less dialogue. Women's dreams more often set indoors and men's dreams are more often set outdoors.

Do dreams change with age?

Sleep patterns change and dream recall decreases with age. Dreams reflect one's emotional concerns, which change in different stages of life.

Why do dreams communicate in symbols?

Pictures, images, and symbols convey more information than words. Symbols are understood best on an intuitive level.

Why do so many dreams seem troublesome rather than happy?

Studies show that about two-thirds of dreams are unpleasant or negative. This may be because they are one of the primary ways people confront and solve problems.

Why do some dreams repeat?

Repeating dreams call attention to something the dreamer needs to change. Resolving the issue usually brings an end to the repetition.

Do the blind dream?

Blind people dream but not necessarily with visual imagery. Their dream content includes the other senses, primarily hearing, as well as emotional tones.

Do animals dream?

The answer to that isn't known. Animals twitch and make noises during sleep as though they are dreaming. Throughout history, people have assumed that animals dream. The Greek philosopher Aristotle and the Roman historian Pliny believed so, and much later Charles Darwin said dogs, cats, horses, and the "higher animals" can dream.

species. The implicate order is the seamless whole of the universe, the unbroken continuum of all things. It is a deep level of reality that contains all time and yet is timeless. It holds all potentiality. It is fluid. From the implicate order unfolds the explicate order, which is what we know as our physical reality. There is a constant flow of energy between the two orders.

Ullman said that the wisdom that flows into our dreams may come from the implicate order: the infinite source. Dreams may be a bridge into the explicate order, or physical reality as part of our evolution.

One thing is clear from scientific research: Dreaming is necessary to maintain physical health. In controlled laboratory experiments, people prevented from REM dreaming become anxious or even panicky, fatigued, irritable, and have difficulty concentrating and remembering. If deprived of sleep long enough, they eventually dream while awake, that is, they hallucinate. When finally allowed their REM sleep, their brains compensate for lost time by greatly increasing the percentage of sleep spent in the REM stage.

Another possible biological function of dreaming relates to the body's maintenance of the proper balance of hormones. During REM sleep, there are higher levels of hormones in the body than at other times. Some neurons are dormant during REM, and this period may function to restore and replenish them.

During NREM sleep great amounts of growth hormone, which is responsible for body tissue renewal, enter the bloodstream. REM sleep may aid in brain tissue renewal.

The healing and diagnostic powers of dreams are explored in Chapter 8.

The Virtual Reality
of Lucid Dreaming

Dreaming is usually a passive activity. Dreams happen automatically. The dreamer does not cause a dream to happen and does not control it. **Lucid dreaming** is different: It is the awareness that one is dreaming while the dream is occurring, sometimes combined with the ability to control the dream. Lucid dreams are the virtual reality of all dreams, a landscape where the strange is real and the real is strange.

Lucid dreaming has been recognized since ancient times. There are different levels of **lucidity**, from a simple awareness of being in a dream to completely controlling the events and outcome of a dream. Some people have a lucid dream every now and then, and others have lucid dreams almost nightly.

In ancient times lucid dreams were valued because they could be used in magic, or as direct ways to reach the gods. Healing dreams incubated at the great dream temples were often lucid. In modern times lucid dreams are believed to be an advanced dreaming skill that people can learn for the purposes of creativity and healing.

Lucid dreams overlap with **astral travel** dreams and also psychic dreams. A lucid dream may feel like an out-of-body trip or may look into the future. People usually enjoy lucid dreaming because they experience a sense of great freedom and power.

HISTORY

The term "lucid dream" did not come into being until the turn of the twentieth century. The term was created by Frederik Willem van Eeden, a Dutch psychiatrist. Prior to that, lucid dreams were known by their unusual characteristics or were simply called dreams.

The earliest known written account of lucid dreaming in Western history is contained in a letter written in 415 by St. Augustine, a pagan who was converted to Christianity and became one of the most important fathers of the early Christian church. In the letter Augustine described the lucid dream of a physician, Gennadius, who lived in Carthage. Gennadius had two dreams in which a spirit guide in the guise of a young man took him to a beautiful city and lectured him about the truth of life after death.[1]

Lucid dreams, as well as dreams in general, lost their importance in the development of Christianity. Instead, they found their place in occultism and alchemy. Lucid dreaming is important in Islamic mysticism and in the complex dream traditions of Buddhism and Hinduism. Tibetan Buddhism has a sophisticated dream yoga in which the yogi learns to have lucid dreams at will in order to understand the illusions of both waking and dreaming states.

When psychology and psychical research emerged in the late nineteenth century, dreams and lucid dreams became the subjects of study. The Marquis d'Hervey de Saint-Denys, a French professor of Chinese literature and language, documented more than two decades of experiments he conducted in learning how to control his dreams. Sigmund Freud acknowledged the existence of lucid dreams but had little to say about them. Carl G. Jung not only acknowledged lucid dreams, he had many of them himself. For Jung, dreams were an important tool for exploring the psyche.

The fields of parapsychology (the modern term for psychical research) and psychology brought renewed attention to all kinds of dreaming. Modern scientific interest in lucid dreams was stimulated in the late 1960s, especially by the publication of books such as *Lucid*

Dreaming (1968) by Celia Green, an overview of the history of lucid dreams. For the most part the scientific establishment has been skeptical about lucid dreams, believing them to be either impossible or else part of occultism. Nonetheless, interest grew in scientific study and testing of lucid dreams.

The state of lucid dreaming was demonstrated in the laboratory in 1970s in independent studies conducted on both sides of the Atlantic. Lucid dreamers were able to give signals with special eye movements during REM stages of sleep, thus demonstrating that they were asleep and aware at the same time.

Lucid dream research is conducted internationally. Stephen LaBerge is one of the leading researchers in the field and is founder of The Lucidity Institute in Palo Alto, California. As a result of studies done by LaBerge and others in the 1970s, many scientists changed their minds about the possibility of lucid dreaming.

Researchers found that lucid dreamers repeatedly could communicate with the outside world by moving their eyes in certain ways while they were in lucid dream states. In all cases the dreamers were in REM stages of sleep when these signals were given. Thus, it was possible for scientists to chart the physiological changes associated with dreaming.[2]

LaBerge's subjects were measured to show correlations between actions in their lucid dreams and physiological changes in their bodies and in brain wave activity. Dreamers were given tasks to perform, which were then measured during their dreaming sleep. According to LaBerge, lucid dreaming thus opened the way for new approaches to mind–body relationships.[3]

Lucid dream studies have demonstrated that some, but not all, individuals can learn how to cause themselves to dream lucidly or can increase their control over their lucid dreams. Research shows that women who meditate may be more likely to have lucid dreams than men who meditate and that people who are easily hypnotized are more likely to dream lucidly. People who have had near-death experiences (NDEs), which share many characteristics with lucid dreams, also have more lucid dreams than other people.

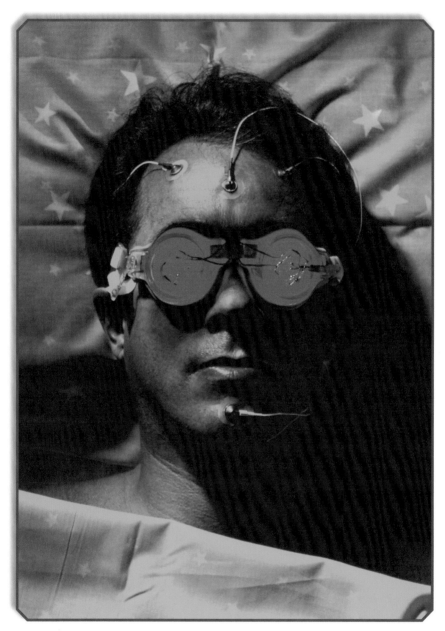

Figure 4.1 *Dr. Steven LaBerge wears goggles that help him recognize when he is in REM sleep, the best state for lucid dreaming. LaBerge, founder of The Lucidity Institute, is a leading lucid-dream researcher.* (Louie Psihoyos/Science Faction/ Corbis)

Slightly more than half of the adult population has at least one lucid dream during life, and about 21 percent have more than one lucid dream each month. LaBerge's subjects report that with practice, they can increase the number of lucid dreams they experience on a regular basis. Those who experience lucid dreams believe that the skill of lucid dreaming can be applied to creativity, problem solving, relationships, health, and getting rid of nightmares.

There may be other, more mysterious sides to lucid dreams as well. Physicist Fred Alan Wolf has suggested that lucid dreams—and maybe dreams in general—are visits to parallel universes: small holograms within a larger cosmic hologram. Wolf calls the ability to lucid dream "parallel universe awareness."

Some lucid dreams seem like mystical experiences, involving a sense of connection, or oneness with, the divine. These lucid dreams often feature spiritual figures such as angels, saints, guides, and divine beings. Some modern researchers believe these dreams are signs of the spiritual evolution of humanity. Perhaps their purpose is to gently introduce people to realms in other dimensions.

CHARACTERISTICS OF LUCID DREAMS

How does one know he or she is dreaming while experiencing a dream? The answers are not always obvious. Lucid dreamers experience certain conditions that clue them in to real-time dream awareness. Here are 10 of them.

1   *Knowing a dream is progress.* The dreamer realizes that he or she is in a dream while it is happening. The realization may come in a false awakening. The dreamer thinks he or she wakes up, while in fact he or she is still dreaming.

2   *The ability to change the course of a dream.* Lucidity enables dreamers to control their dreams in different ways. Sometimes dreamers can decide exactly what is going to happen, such as the actions of themselves and other characters in a dream. They can also rewrite

Dream Tech

People vary in their ability to have lucid dreams. Some people have lucid dreams almost every night, while others have them infrequently. Researchers have learned how to teach people to increase the number and frequency of their lucid dreams, usually by following the trial-and-error mental experiments recorded by dreamers throughout history.

For about the past 50 years, people have also experimented with technological devices that supposedly provide that extra helping hand better than any visualization or thought process. Some of the devices for aiding lucid dreaming are:

Masks and goggles. These devices are designed to alert a sleeping person when he or she starts to dream, usually by detecting the fluttering of their eyelids during rapid eye movement (REM) sleep. When those stages occur, the masks either flash soft lights or make sounds through tiny speakers. The cues are not supposed to wake the person completely, but alert them to a dreaming state. The idea is that the dreamer can deliberately gain lucidity or awareness in the dream.

Headphones. These pump in brain wave entrainment signals, such as pulses of sound that are designed to alter states of consciousness. The sounds help a dreamer stay in a prolonged state of borderland sleep. Through this method it is hoped that lucid dreams will be more likely to occur.

Hypnosis. Tape or CD recordings of hypnotic suggestions are played while falling asleep. The suggestions instruct the dreamer to become lucid while dreaming and to remember the dreams upon awakening.

Do dream tech devices work? Results are as varied as the natural abilities of dreamers. Some dreamers say their success rates dramatically increase, while others say the devices do not work well, or not at all, for them. Bottom line: An individual simply doesn't know until he or she tries them.

dreams they don't like. Not all lucid dreamers have total control. Sometimes it is possible to alter only a small part of a dream.

3   *The ability to feel physical sensation.* Touching objects in a lucid dream feels as real as it does in waking life.

4   *Unusual abilities and actions.* Lucid dreamers often feel weightless. They fly, float, and levitate.

5   *A strange "atmosphere."* Lucid dreams have a different "feel" to them. For example, the atmosphere may feel heavy, like being underwater, or else have an electrical quality, like the supercharged air just before a thunderstorm.

6   *Brilliant light.* Lucid dreams may be flooded with intense white light, sometimes enough to make dreamers squint or shield their eyes.

7   *Vivid colors.* Colors in lucid dreams are exaggerated. They are exceptionally bright, sometimes fluorescent. Some lucid dreamers say the colors are "not of this world."

8   *Intense emotions.* Like colors, emotions are exaggerated and heightened. Lucid dreamers report feelings of euphoria and excitement.

9   *Mental sharpness.* Lucid dreamers feel they have increased brainpower and are able to understand complex things and find solutions to problems.

10   *Out-of-body sensations.* Strange sounds in the ears, such as ringing, roaring, and buzzing, as well as electrical sensations in the body, are sometimes experienced at the start of lucid dreaming. People who have out-of-body experiences report the same sensations.

While these characteristics appear in many lucid dreams, they do not guarantee a lucid dream. All lucid dreamers must learn over time what signals a lucid dream to them.

HOW TO HAVE A LUCID DREAM

Lucid dreamers experiment to find the best ways to encourage lucid dreaming. Many find that meditation before going to sleep is one of the best techniques. They quiet their minds and concentrate on an intention to have and remember a lucid dream: "I will have a lucid dream tonight and I will remember it when I wake up." It is necessary to relax one's body as much as possible and focus on calm breathing. Let go of thoughts about the day.

Another technique is to decide on a symbol that will help awaken one to lucidity whenever it appears in a dream. For example, one might say, "Whenever I see a dove, then I know I am dreaming." The symbol should be something that will stand out and be noticed.

Some people discover that sleeping in certain positions is helpful; these vary according to individuals. Sleeping on one's back or on either side is more successful for most than sleeping on the stomach.

Some lucid dreamers experiment with techniques for WILDs, or Wake-Initiated Lucid Dreaming. Some prefer to sleep first, then wake up and focus on having a lucid dream through self-suggestion. Others have more success during the day at times when they feel like taking naps. Discussions and tips for all kinds of lucid dreaming can be found on The Lucidity Institute's Web site, http://www.lucidity.com.

WAYS TO STAY LUCID

One of the most difficult aspects of lucid dreaming is staying in the dream. For many dreamers, as soon as they realize they are lucid, the dream ends. Researchers have learned a few methods of retaining lucidity that work for many people.

1 *Focus on something solid.* Focus on an object, the ground, or the body. Touch something solid. Hold your hands up in front of you.

2 *Spin around.* This is a favorite technique of LaBerge. As he or she spins, the dreamer should say, "The next object I encounter will be in the dream," and then stop spinning.

3 *Stay calm.* It's exciting to be in a lucid dream, but the heightened emotion may actually be a dream killer. One way to stay calm is to repeat, "This is a dream" or "I am dreaming."

WHAT TO DO IN A LUCID DREAM

The first thing to do in a lucid dream is direct the action, which will be determined by the dream itself. It is fun to experiment by trying to levitate or fly. With practice, lucid dreamers attempt more complicated tasks. They may ask for a creative idea or a solution to a problem. They may visit specific places and people on earth or travel around in other dimensions. They may seek to be healed of fears, phobias, injuries, and illnesses.

Researchers and lucid dreamers agree that it is important to act responsibly and not do anything in the dream world that would not be proper in the waking world.

Lucid dreaming is one of the most exciting frontiers in dream research. By studying lucid dreams, people may learn more about the reasons for dreams and how dreams work.

Night Flying

In biblical lore Enoch is the son of Jared and the seventh descendant of Adam and Eve. One day he takes a nap on his couch and has a mind-bending experience. A "great distress" comes into his heart. It seems that he wakes up. Enoch is startled to see two huge beings in front of him. They are angels in the guise of men, shining like the sun, with eyes like burning lamps and lips that emit fire. They are whiter than snow, with wings brighter than gold.

The angels inform Enoch that they have been sent by God to take him on a trip. He goes out of his body and rides on the wings of the angels up to heaven.

There, Enoch is given the tour of all tours and sees every level of heaven, the angels in them, and the souls of the dead. He is told about the creation of the world and all things and is shown the future. Enoch is instructed to write it all down, and he takes furious dictation from an angel named Pravuil. He is returned to earth with orders to teach others what he has been shown.

Three versions of the book of Enoch are known to have been written. Each one tells a different version of the same story and what Enoch saw in the heavens. Although credited to Enoch, they were probably written by different writers between the second century BCE and the sixth century CE.

The ancient writers did not use terms like astral travel or out-of-body experience, but the description of Enoch's adventure is similar to astral journeys described today. In modern terms Enoch did some astral traveling while dreaming a lucid dream. He experienced a "false awakening," thinking he awakened to see the angels, when in fact they were part of his lucid dream.

Throughout history, people have had amazing journeys in various states of sleep. They wake up wondering whether the experience was real or only a dream. The ancients believed their dreams were real experiences in their own right, a belief that continues in many cultures around the world today.

Who are some other spectacular astral travelers?

EMANUEL SWEDENBORG

Emanuel Swedenborg (1688–1772) was a Swedish scientist and mystic who took numerous astral trips to heaven and hell. He communicated with God, angels, and demons. He described in great detail the organization of the afterlife. He believed that people choose their own heaven or hell based on their choices and actions in life.

Swedenborg was well educated and was an inventor. He worked on designs for submarines, air guns, and even flying machines. He also worked as an assessor in the mining industry. His life changed suddenly in 1743 when he began having ecstatic visions. He was overcome with revelations about heaven and hell, the work of angels and spirits, the true meaning of the Bible, and the order of the universe.

The experiences took place in the borderland states between sleep and wakefulness, either as he was going to sleep or as he was awakening. In this twilight state of consciousness, he found himself transported to other realms and able to talk to the dead and spirits. Swedenborg called these visionary travels being "in the spirit." He knew that he was out of his body.

Although the experiences took place in a state of semi-sleep, he maintained that he was fully aware of what he was doing. Over time,

Figure 5.1 *Swedish scientist, philosopher, and religious mystic Emanuel Swedenborg gave extensive accounts of his experiences with astral travel.* (Getty Images)

he learned how to astral travel at will and not depend on the sleep state. He used his breathing to begin and control his journeys. He could remain out-of-body for up to three days at a time.

Swedenborg believed that angels cause our dreams and that the images in dreams reflect the thoughts and feelings of angels. Convinced that God had selected him to be his spiritual emissary, he quit his job in 1747 to devote himself fully to his visionary work. He recorded his astral experiences in 30 books, all written in Latin.

Swedenborg said that immediately after death, the soul goes to an intermediary state called the "spiritual world" or the "world of the spirits," halfway between earth and heaven and hell. The soul awakens in an environment similar to the one it left behind. This is called "first state." It is the first of three states, and it lasts for a few days. Angels, friends, and relatives come to greet the newcomer. If a spouse has preceded the newly arrived soul, they may reunite.

The first state is followed by second state in which the soul undergoes an intense self-examination. In the third state, wicked souls go to hell and good souls go to heaven, where they prepare to become angels.

Swedenborg's ideas were controversial in his day and have remained so to present times, even though he has many followers. A church was founded on his philosophy. Whether or not people agree with him, the record of his dreamy astral travels is a fascinating example of the mysterious realms that lie beyond wakefulness.

OLIVER FOX

Englishman Oliver Fox (1885–1949), born Hugh G. Callaway, was a sickly child and spent a great deal of time in bed. However, he did not experience astral travel until adulthood, when he had spontaneous experiences during lucid dreaming. With practice he learned how to recognize that he was dreaming, by having a false awakening, and then to direct his astral travel. He called his astral travel dreams the "Dream of Knowledge."[1]

Fox experimented heavily in astral travel dreaming between 1902 and 1938. He improved his techniques, learning how to astral travel while in a drowsy state before falling asleep. His body felt as though it was sleeping, but his mind was alert. Then Fox was able to astral project himself out of his body entirely without the "Dream of Knowledge."

Fox viewed his lucid dream world as comparable to the **astral plane**, an invisible level of reality that exists next to the physical world. His "Dream of Knowledge" was characterized by a sensation of atmospheric changes, which he described as the pressurized feeling that builds before an electrical storm.

He experienced flying and levitation; telepathy with others; religious visions, such as seeing the figure of Christ (which he decided was a thought-form, not the real Christ); and precognition (he viewed a test prior to his taking it, and correctly saw two questions that would be asked).

His adventures abruptly came to an end when one day he found himself unable to project out of his body. Consulting a medium, he was told that higher spiritual powers had ended his travels because they said he was becoming too attuned to psychic forces that might sweep him away before his work in his physical body on earth was completed.

Fox's astral travels autobiography, *Astral Projection: A Record of Out-of-the-Body Experiences,* was published around 1938.

SYLVAN MULDOON

Sylvan Muldoon (1907–1971) also was a sickly child who spent a lot of time in bed. At age 12, he suddenly began having out-of-body experiences (OBEs). His first experience occurred during a visit to a spiritualist camp with his mother.

Muldoon researched astral travel from 1915 to 1950. He traveled about in a double of his physical body. He believed that dreams of falling and flying corresponded to movements during astral travel. Many of his OBEs began with flying dreams. He had the best results when he fasted. He believed that the lack of food encouraged his double to separate more easily from his physical body because it needed energy and went out to search for a source.[2] Like other dream travelers, Muldoon eventually learned how to project himself out of his body at will, and without being dependent upon sleeping and dreaming.

Figure 5.2 *American researcher Sylvan Muldoon was an authority on out-of-body experiences and astral travel.* (Mary Evans Picture Library/The Image Works)

He wrote of his research and experiences in *The Projection of the Astral Body* (1936), co-authored with the prominent psychical researcher Hereward Carrington. As Muldoon's health improved, his astral travel became less frequent.

ROBERT MONROE

In 1958 an American radio and television executive named Robert A. Monroe (1915–1995) began astral traveling spontaneously while relaxed and near sleep. Monroe had incredible experiences not limited to the earth plane, but reaching to realms including the transition plane between life and the afterlife. He had contact with dead people and nonhuman beings. Like Fox, he conducted his own research, which led to his writing several books and establishing The Monroe Institute in Faber, Virginia. Monroe developed his own techniques for launching astral travel using guided meditation and sound.

Monroe's first astral travel experiences began when he would lie down to go to sleep. Before he reached sleep—when he was in the hypnagogic stage—he would experience a buzzing and vibrating and feel himself lift out of his body. Like an explorer touching the shores of an unknown land, Monroe explored and mapped the astral realm.

He described an astonishing range of experiences, both pleasant and unpleasant, in which he encountered other beings, some of whom were helpful to him; demonic or subhuman entities and thought-forms that attacked him; a benevolent energy presence of overwhelming magnitude (he does not say whether or not it was "God"); and the astral bodies of other humans. Monroe found that the relaxed state of presleep, the hypnagogic state, is an ideal medium for astral traveling. The key is developing the ability to hold onto lucidity instead of falling asleep. He named this "mind awake/ body asleep."

He found that a specific sleeping posture helped him to attain this state. He called it "rotation" or "peel-off." He would lie on his back, and as he dropped into sleep, he would slowly turn over without using his arms or legs for assistance. When he had turned 180 degrees, he would think of floating up and away.

Monroe found that in his astral double he could pass through solid objects and go instantly to any place that he thought about. At first he tried to stay close to his physical body while he practiced staying in control. Over time he traveled further and further out. He identified levels of reality he found:

- Locale I is the here-and-now earth plane, people and places in the physical world.

- Locale II is the infinite astral plane, the place where dreams occur, and which incorporates concepts of heaven and hell. Many of the places in this level seem familiar, he said, for they are the creations of

Shared Dreams

Do you think your dreams are private? Not so much as you might wish!

Evidence that dreams overlap has existed since ancient times. Two or more persons can share the same dream, either spontaneously or by deliberate intent.

Today the phenomenon of shared dreams is called **mutual dreaming**. Studies show that about one-third of dreams are shared in some way. The figure may be even higher. Most people do not talk about their dreams, so there are few avenues for discovering whether or not one has shared a dream with someone.

Mutual dreams are more likely to happen between persons who are emotionally linked and living close together, such as spouses and romantic partners, family members, and close friends. They can occur between co-workers, casual acquaintances, and even strangers, though this is less likely.

Shared dreams happen in various degrees.

consciousness and have been mapped and visited by countless souls. Here are the dead as well as nonhuman entities.

- Locale III transcends time and space and appears to be a parallel universe located on the other side of a hole in the space–time continuum. According to Monroe, there are yet unidentified, higher realms beyond our ability to comprehend.

In 1975 Monroe patented a sound wave system called Hemi-Sync (for hemispheric synchronization), which balances the right and left hemispheres of the brain and which is used in The Monroe Institute training systems.

All of these famous night fliers felt they traveled somewhere beyond the physical earth. Where exactly did they go?

1 *Mutual recognition.* Two or more dreamers see and recognize each other in their dreams, even though the dream action may not be similar.

2 *Mutual dream elements.* Objects, settings, actions, dialogue, and other details are the same or similar in shared dreams.

3 *Shared plot, different characters.* The dreams are similar in plot and action, but do not necessarily include the other dreamers.

4 *Lucidity and out-of-body experience.* Dreamers experience each other in lucid circumstances or initiate OBEs together in dreams.

5 *Precognition.* Dreamers see the same future event.

Some researchers, including Linda Lane Magallon, the author of *Mutual Dreaming* (1997), think that mutual dreaming may reveal how human beings are connected to each other in a universal way.[3] One of the best ways to discover if one is sharing mutual dreams is to compare dreams on a regular basis with family and friends or join a dream group.

6

The Astral World

Where do people go when they dream? Is there a single destination or many destinations? The ancients believed that dreaming involved literal travel to another place where the rules of time and space are different. Many modern scientists believe that no travel is involved in dreaming. Rather, dream images are served up like movies from the subconscious mind. On the other hand, many dreamers feel they are definitely out of their bodies when they dream. Out-of-body experiences also can occur during waking consciousness, especially in meditation. In either dreams or wakefulness, people may have the feeling of being out of the body without actually seeing it or they may see their own sleeping body.

Dream researchers distinguish OBE dreams from lucid dreams. Stephen LaBerge's studies have indicated that about 9 percent of lucid dreams also are OBE dreams. It is often difficult for many dreamers to draw a line between the two: OBE dreams are lucid and lucid dreams involve OBEs. The feeling of being out of body may be more pronounced in some lucid dreams than in others. For example, a dreamer may be specifically aware of leaving and reentering his or her body. In other cases, a dreamer may simply know he or she is outside the body at the same time as realizing he or she is lucid dreaming.

The frequent out-of-body traveler Oliver Fox reported that he rarely saw his own body, though he often saw the sleeping body of his wife. Both Fox and Sylvan Muldoon concluded that out-of-body projections vary according to the individual.

Dream traveling is the visiting of distant places while asleep. The places may be on earth or in other realms. Dream traveling may be marked by sensations of flying and varying degrees of lucidity.

THE ASTRAL PLANE

If travel is involved in dreaming, it may occur on the astral plane. Since ancient times this has been described as an otherworldly place, but it has not necessarily been called "the astral plane." People have visited there without dreaming, through spontaneous and deliberate OBEs.

According to descriptions, the astral plane is a level of existence that lies next to the physical world but is invisible. The astral plane has no natural landscape of its own. It is white, formless, and very fluid. Duplicates of everything in the physical world exist on the astral plane. It is inhabited with duplicates of ourselves that appear as figures in our dreams, and by other beings. Although astral forms are duplicates, they look shadowy, like phantoms. Nothing on the astral plane is completely solid.

THE ASTRAL BODY

Traveling to the astral plane and realms beyond is done in a vehicle called the **astral body**, an exact duplicate of the physical body. The astral body has been called by different names. Sylvan Muldoon called the astral body the "soul body." Robert A. Monroe, who became famous for his out-of-body journeys, called the astral body the "second body." His own second body appeared as a bright, glowing outline duplicating the physical. It could register touch, and it moved according to his thought. The astral body passes through the solid objects in physical reality, such as walls, ceilings, mountains, and so forth. It is not affected by the elements.[1]

Figure 6.1 *The astral body leaves the physical body during astral travel.*
(O. Burriel/Photo Researchers, Inc.)

The astral body stays connected to the physical body by the **astral cord**, a silver cord that resembles an elastic, umbilical cord of infinite length. It joins the two bodies at the heads: the forehead of the physical form and the back of the skull of the astral form. The astral cord has been described by such terms as "a coil of light," "a luminous garden-hose," "a strong ray of light," "a lighted cord," and "a tail of light."

References to the astral cord appear in ancient writings of the Egyptians, Indians, and Chinese, and in Greece. It is mentioned in Ecclesiastes 12:6-7: "Remember Him before the silver cord is broken and the golden bowl is crushed, the pitcher by the well is shattered and the wheel at the cistern is crushed; then the dust will return to the earth as it was, and the spirit will return to God who gave it." The verses refer to paying attention to spiritual matters before life is ended.

The cord allows the astral body to range anywhere in the universe. The closer the astral body is to the physical body, the thicker the cord. According to esoteric tradition, the astral cord enables the astral body to rejoin the physical body. When a person dies, the cord is cut.

Muldoon observed that breath travels from the astral to the physical via the astral cord. "You breathe in the Astral, and your heart beats in the Astral. . . . Your physical heart beats because within it the Astral heart beats," he said. "Each breath taken in the Astral can be seen pulsing over the 'cord' and causes a duplicate breath to be taken by the body."

Many persons who astral travel, whether in dreams or in spontaneous experiences, say they can see the astral cord.

ASTRAL TRAVEL

Astral travel is the ability to journey in the astral body to distant places in an instant. Places include locations on earth, the astral plane, and other realms beyond. Astral travel is sometimes called "astral projection."

The leaving of the physical body is often preceded by strong, high-frequency vibrations. Prior to separation people feel electrical sensations in their body or hear loud buzzing, roaring, or ringing sounds. These sensations can occur in lucid dreams and become part of the dream.

Individuals leave their bodies through their head or solar plexus or by rising up and floating away. The physical body appears to be sleeping or in a coma-like state. Consciousness remains connected to the body via the astral cord. Reentry is accomplished by returning through the head or solar plexus or by melting back into the body.

There are many descriptions of journeying to other realms in ancient literature. The ancient Egyptians described a *ba*, or soul-like essence that manifested outside the body during sleep and after death. It was often portrayed as a bird with a human head. The *ka* was the vital essence, a collective energy that was part of every individual and which could be projected outward.

Around the seventh century BCE, the Greeks adopted an Eastern concept of out-of-body travel during sleep. This concept was embraced by the Greek religious movement called Orphism,

Going to Astral School

Ordinary dreams of going to school are common, but sometimes the classroom or teaching institution seems out of this world. Many dreamers feel that they travel to the astral plane to attend class for spiritual instruction.

Michael Talbot, the author of *The Holographic Universe* and *The Reincarnation Handbook,* had astral school dreams often. He gave this description:

> Throughout my high school and college years I had vivid and frequent dreams that I was attending classes on spiritual subjects at a strangely beautiful university in some sublime and other worldly place. These were not anxiety dreams about going to school, but incredibly pleasant flying dreams in which I floated weightlessly to lectures on the human energy field and reincarnation. During these dreams I sometimes encountered people I had known in this life but who had died, and even people who identified themselves as souls about to be reborn. Intriguingly, I have met several other individuals, usually people with more than normal psychic ability, who had also had these dreams. One, a talented Texas clairvoyant . . . was so baffled by the experience that he often asked his nonplussed mother why he had to go to school *twice,* once during the day with all the other children, and once at night while he slept.[2]

Is it possible that people get an education in dreams that they could not get in an earthly classroom? Dreamers who have these experiences must decide for themselves.

which influenced many of Greece's later great thinkers, including Pythagoras and Plato.

Following the thread of Orphic thought, Plato called dreams "the between state," a real place where the human soul went during sleep to meet the gods and demigods who are otherwise inaccessible. He said that dreams are another way to know the world besides sense and experience; people can receive "the inspired word" of the divine in their sleep. Socrates, Pliny, and Plotinus gave descriptions of experiences that resemble astral travel; Plotinus wrote of being "lifted out of the body into myself" on many occasions. Plutarch described an astral projection that occurred to Aridanaeus in 79 CE.

Saints and mystics recorded their astral travel experiences, usually to the heavens to have conversations with divine figures. In the Eastern mystical traditions techniques are taught in the yogas (spiritual and philosophical disciplines) for mastering astral travel.

WHAT DREAMERS DO DURING ASTRAL TRAVEL

Sometimes astral travel dreams seem like adventures for fun: There are sensations of flying and of visiting places on earth and "somewhere else." Dreamers experiment with passing through solid objects such as doors and furniture, levitating, flying, and moving objects.

Sometimes dreamers feel they are summoned by higher spiritual forces, who may remain hidden, to perform certain tasks. Monroe said that sometimes he was called or drawn by a signal or energy that pulled him to another location, where he found another person in need of help. For example, he met newly deceased souls who had arrived in the astral plane but were not aware that they were dead. They needed to be gently informed of their passage out of physical life and redirected into the afterlife.

The Psychic Side of Dreams

One night in August 2001, a man in Iowa has a terrifying nightmare. He dreams that a plane crashes into a tall building somewhere and many people die. The dream is so vivid and realistic that it seems like a real event. The next morning, he searches the news headlines, half expecting to see his dream played out. He is relieved there was no such tragedy, and it was "only a dream."

The dream happens in real life, however—but not until September 11, 2001, when terrorists crash two jumbo passenger jets into the World Trade Center towers in New York City. The buildings collapse, and several thousand people die.

The man in Iowa previewed the disaster in a psychic dream. He had plenty of company; many others dreamed vivid details about 9/11 in advance. They dreamed about the World Trade Center, the plane that hit the Pentagon, and the plane that crashed near Shanksville, Pennsylvania. The dreams were filled with scenes that later took place: planes crashing into buildings, planes crashing on the ground, tall buildings collapsing, flames shooting out of buildings, people running covered in gray ash, and feelings of panic, mass death, and war. These nightmarish dreams were so realistic that many people awoke from them in terror and sweat.

Examples of some of the dreams reported in the weeks after 9/11 were:

I dreamed that chaos and destruction had erupted. It seemed like the end of the world. There was a gray film over everything, like a nuclear winter. People were running all over.

I was in a city where a tall building was on fire. People were screaming in the windows, and some were jumping.

A plane fell out of the sky into a city. I seemed to be watching from above and far away. I just knew that there were a lot of people dead. I felt awful.

Other dreamers reported dreams in which they felt a vague sense of dread that "something terrible" was going to happen soon.

While these dreams captured elements of the 9/11 terrorist attacks, few of the dreamers knew they were previewing a specific future event. A dream that a tall building is collapsing would not have sparked the immediate connection that terrorists were going to fly planes into the World Trade Center on the morning of September 11, 2001. The dreams simply seemed nightmarish, disturbing, and unusual in the course of "normal dreaming." Only after the events took place were the dreamers able to match the dream to the circumstances.

PRECOGNITION DREAMS

A dream that previews coming events is a **precognition**, or direct knowing of the future. **Precognitive dreaming** has been reported since ancient times. They are the most common psychic dreams. Precognition alone can occur in a variety of ways, including visions during waking hours. According to studies by parapsychologists, most precognitions—60 to 70 percent—occur in dreams.[1] Dreams seem to be efficient carriers for psychic, or psi, information, such as knowledge of future events. No one knows for certain why. One possible explanation is that when people are asleep, their minds can access information outside of linear time.

Studies have also shown that most precognitive dreams happen within 24 to 48 hours of the actual event. It is possible, however, to dream of events months in advance.

No one knows why some people have precognitive dreams and others do not. Precognitive dreams do not depend upon a person's psychic ability or their personal relationship to the event. While many precognitive dreams do deal with things about to happen to an individual's family and friends, some concern big events, such as large-scale disasters, that emotionally shock a large number of people. Famous examples of precognitive dreams about shocking events involve the assassinations of important people.

Calpurnia, the wife of Roman Emperor Julius Caesar, had a dream in which Roman senators stabbed a statue of her husband with knives, and blood flowed from the statue. She did not know that several senators were indeed plotting to kill her husband. Nonetheless, Calpurnia awakened certain that her husband would be killed that very day in the public Forum. Caesar was skeptical and told a senator, Decius, about Calpurnia's dream. Decius was one of the conspirators. He told Caesar the dream was a favorable omen about future Roman victories. Caesar went to the Forum as planned that day—and was stabbed to death by his enemies.

Around April 1865 President Abraham Lincoln had an eerie dream forecasting his own death. He wrote:

> About ten days ago, I retired very late. I had been up waiting for important dispatches from the front. I could not have been long in bed when I fell into a slumber, for I was weary. I soon began to dream. There seemed to be a death-like stillness about me. Then I heard subdued sobs, as if a number of people were weeping. I thought I left my bed and wandered downstairs. There the silence was broken by the same pitiful sobbing, but the mourners were invisible. I went from room to room; no living person was in sight, but the same mournful sounds of distress met

me as I passed along. I saw light in all the rooms; every object was familiar to me; but where were all the people who were grieving as if their hearts would break? I was puzzled and alarmed. What could be the meaning of all this? Determined to find the cause of a state of things so mysterious and so shocking, I kept on until I arrived at the East Room, which I entered. There I met with a sickening surprise. Before me was a catafalque, on which rested a corpse wrapped in funeral vestments. Around it were stationed soldiers who were acting as guards; and there was a throng of people, gazing mournfully upon the corpse, whose face was covered, others weeping pitifully. "Who is dead in the White House?" I demanded of one of the soldiers, "The President," was his answer; "he was killed by an assassin." Then came a loud burst of grief from the crowd, which woke me from my dream. I slept no more that night; and although it was only a dream, I have been strangely annoyed by it ever since.

On April 14 Lincoln was shot to death by John Wilkes Booth at Ford's Theater. His body was laid out for a wake in the East Room of the White House, just as he had seen in his dream.

On June 28, 1914, the assassination of Austria's Archduke Franz Ferdinand and his wife ignited political tensions that set off World War I. The night before they were killed, the former tutor of the archduke, Bishop Joseph Lanyi of Grosswardein, Hungary, dreamed about the assassination almost exactly as it happened. The couple was shot as they rode in an open car in a motorcade. Lanyi made a sketch of his dream. The sketch matched a photograph taken at the scene and published in newspapers.

Besides assassinations, there have been precognitive dreams reported prior to airplane crashes, train wrecks, fires, natural disasters, highway accidents, and other calamities. In most cases the events happen, anyway. Sometimes, however, precognitive dreams may have helped individuals avoid a disaster, as in the case of the sinking of the *Titanic* on its maiden voyage in 1912.

As long as two weeks before the supposedly unsinkable ship sailed out of England on April 10, people who were planning to be aboard had warning dreams or bad feelings that the ship was "doomed."[2] Some of those persons canceled their plans, among them the American financier J. Pierpont Morgan. He officially canceled his trip for business reasons. However, Morgan was a financier of the ship, and was enthusiastic about being present on its maiden voyage. It is not known whether or not he had a dream or negative feelings combined with a dream. The ship sailed without a full passenger load, which was unusual considering the advance publicity given the superliner. On April 12, the ship hit an iceberg and sank, killing 1,502 of the 2,207 aboard. Similarly, when the *Empress of Ireland* sank in the Lawrence River in 1914, its first-class cabins were two-thirds empty and its second-class accomodations half-empty.

What made people stay away from these particular voyages? People may have paid attention to psychic warnings through dreams and **premonitions**. It is difficult for researchers to pinpoint origins, because bad feelings in dreams may combine with bad feelings in waking consciousness. Much depends on the extent to which an individual pays attention to dreams. It may never be possible to separate dream intuition from waking intuition.

In the 1960s researcher W.E. Cox examined rail passenger loads on American trains that had accidents between 1950–1955. He found a remarkable drop-off in average passenger counts on some, but not all, accident days. Cox concluded that many people who had intended to travel on disaster-bound trains may have unconsciously, or for some unusual reason, altered their plans or missed the trains by being late.[3] He was not able to interview people about why they made their travel choices, but the unexplained and significant drop in passenger loads suggested intuitive or psychic feelings that influenced travel. Some of these uneasy feelings were likely to have been transmitted in dreams.

Plenty of anecdotal testimony exists that people do dream the future or at least pieces of it. For example, on February 1, 2003, the *Columbia* space shuttle broke apart minutes from its scheduled landing in Florida, killing the seven astronauts aboard. The meteor-like disintegration of the craft 60 miles up in the morning sky played on television to shocked audiences. Once again, many dreamers realized after the fact that they had had precognitive elements in dreams concerning this tragedy, but like the 9/11 attacks, no one had the whole picture. Once again, people regretted not foreseeing enough to perhaps prevent the disaster.

Perhaps the most famous precognitive dream about an airplane disaster is the tragic crash of American Airlines Flight 191 in 1979. On May 25 a DC-10 jumbo jet with 270 people aboard took off from Chicago's O'Hare airfield bound for Los Angeles. On takeoff one of the massive engines fell off the plane, and the second engine shut down. The plane was 500 feet in the air when it turned radically on its side with one wing tilted up, and then fell to the earth. Everyone aboard was killed. At the time, it was the worst air disaster in the United States.

This accident was seen in advance in vivid detail in precognitive dreams of at least two people, who alerted others in advance of the impending disaster. Unfortunately, there was not enough information to avert the accident. In the aftermath of the tragedy the same questions arose about the purpose of precognitive dreaming as arose more than 20 years later after 9/11 and *Columbia*. If people get advance warning of a future event, why do they not get enough information to change course? If a disaster or undesirable event can't be prevented, what is the purpose of psychic dreaming?

One of the dreamers of Flight 191 was a New York woman who had a history of precognitive dreaming, and had accurately predicted other air disasters. In 1978 she had dreamed in advance of another famous disaster that occurred that September. A PSA jetliner with 144 people aboard, en route from Los Angeles to San Diego, was near landing when it collided with a private plane and plunged to the ground in flames. Everyone aboard the jetliner was killed, as well as the two people aboard the private plane. In her dream there was a plane in the sky headed for California; the dream was permeated with a feeling of imminent disaster.

The woman, a counselor who made numerous appearances on radio, was on air the next morning in Pine Bluff, Arkansas, where she related her dream. Three hours later, the news of the disaster broke. It was the worst air disaster to date, but would be superseded by the 1979 American Airlines Flight 191 crash.

Less than five months later she began having dreams of another airline disaster, this time in the Midwest. She felt it was still weeks or months away, but she was certain that it would happen. On March 12, she made the prediction on a radio show in Tulsa, Oklahoma. Off the air, she gave the name of the airlines to the show host. It was American Airlines, and the plane would be headed for California.

The woman dreamed again of the impending crash, and gave details on a radio show in Savannah, Georgia, on April 26. It would be a jumbo jet. The accident was less than one month away. However, she was not certain of the exact location where it would happen.

Recurring and disturbing dreams of the accident made her reluctant to fall asleep. She dreamed of being both a passenger on the doomed plane and a spectator to the crash. In the dream, she was a passenger as the plane went down. After the plane crashed and everyone was dead, she walked away as a spectator. At that point, she bolted awake, frightened.[4]

Another significant precognitive dreamer was a man in Ohio, who had no previous experience of psychic dreams. On May 16, 1979, he was jarred awake by a terrifying vision of an airplane crash. In the dream, he was looking out to the right over a field with a diagonal tree line. He looked up into the sky and saw a big jet whose engines were making an unusual noise. He had no sense of danger or impending doom, but then the plane started to turn with its wing pulled way up. It flipped onto its back and dove straight into ground, exploding. As the sound died out, he woke up.

The dream was frightening and unlike any he had ever had. He tried to forget it, but the emotional impact of it and the vividness of the images remained with him throughout the day. The dream repeated a second time. When he awoke, the man found he'd been crying in his sleep. This time he felt a sense of urgency, that he must take action fast. The dream repeated every night. On May 22, after the seventh dream, the man called the local office of the Federal Aviation Administration (FAA). He relayed the dream and said the plane was an American Airlines jet with a big engine on the tail. An FAA official reviewed details with him. But unfortunately, the dream gave no information as to where and when this accident would happen.

On May 25 he had the dream for the 10th time. He awoke with a different feeling. He knew he would never have the dream again. Throughout the day he was upset and distracted, so much so that he left work early at 4 P.M., the very time when the doomed plane was taking off at Chicago (where it was 3 P.M.). The disaster happened as he had witnessed it in his dream. He did not see or know an engine fell off, but witnesses captured dramatic photographs of the plane turned with its wing up before diving into the ground.

When he heard the news, the man knew that the plane crash was his dream. Understandably, he blamed himself for not being able to prevent the accident. He wondered if only he had gotten a little more information, he could have stopped it. He thought he had been singled out as the only person in the whole world to see it in advance. Much later, he still felt the crash could have been prevented, if he or someone else had been able to preview the right information.[5]

No one yet knows how to improve the accuracy of precognitive dreaming in order to make it useful to society. It also would be ideal if people could produce precognitive dreams on demand, instead of waiting for them to happen at random.

Figure 7.1 *Smoke pours from a building where American Airlines Flight 191 crashed just after takeoff on May 25, 1979. A man claimed to have had a total of 10 different dreams that foretold the crash.* (AP Photo)

TELEPATHY DREAMS

The second most common psychic dream involves **telepathy**, the transmission of thoughts from one person to another. Ancient people believed this was possible and used dream telepathy to send messages and entire dreams to targeted recipients.

Sigmund Freud observed that "sleep creates favorable conditions for telepathy," and referred often to dream telepathy in his clinical psychiatric work with patients.

Telepathic dreaming has been of interest to psychical researchers and parapsychologists since the late nineteenth century. The founders of the Society for Psychical Research (SPR) in London collected 149 dream telepathy cases in their study of spontaneous paranormal experiences, published in *Phantasms of the Living* (1886). More than half of the dream telepathy cases involved death, crisis, or distress.

The first known effort to induce telepathic dreams in a controlled experiment was conducted in the late 1800s by an Italian psychical

Can Precognitive Dreams Prevent Disasters?

If people can dream the future, then can dreams about coming disasters be used to prevent those events from taking place? It sounds logical, but in reality, psychic dreams are too unreliable.

On October 21, 1966, a landslide of coal mine waste tumbled down a mountain in Aberfan, Wales, and buried a school, killing 28 adults and 116 children. Up to two weeks beforehand, 200 people experienced precognitions about the disaster, including dreams, visions, and uneasy feelings. One especially chilling precognitive dream was had by a young girl the night before the disaster. In the morning, she told her mother she had dreamed that everyone went to school, but there was no school because "something black had come down all over it." She also told her mother she was not afraid to die, for she would be with two children she knew. Sadly, the girl and the two children she named were killed later that day.

researcher, G.B. Ermacora. He used a medium whose control spirit al-legedly sent telepathic dreams to the medium's four-year-old cousin.

Of all types of psychic dreams, telepathy has proved the easiest to study in the laboratory.

Telepathic dream studies have been conducted in modern times, some by the SPR and the American Society for Psychical Research, as well as by others. An estimated 25 percent of cases of telepathy involve dreams.

The most famous dream telepathy research was conducted in the 1960s by researchers Montague Ullman and Stanley Krippner at the now-defunct Dream Laboratory of the Maimonides Medical Center in Brooklyn, New York. Here is how their research was done. When volunteer subjects were in stages of REM sleep, a person in another

The disaster prompted the founding of the British Premonitions Bureau in 1967. The bureau's purpose was to collect and screen precognitive warnings in an effort to avert other disasters. In 1968 the Central Premonitions Bureau was established in New York City for the same purpose. Both bureaus failed and closed in the 1980s. They failed because precognitive information was never precise enough, as illustrated by the 9/11 dreams that provided no details about when and where the event would occur. Many tips the bureaus received were wrong altogether and about events that never came to pass.

Individuals have reported that precognitive dreams have helped them avoid problems and even tragedies, such as accidents. Large-scale disasters seem to be another matter. Perhaps, as some people believe, such events are destined to happen, no matter what. If so, then many questions are raised about any individual's ability to influence fate. Until researchers better understand the nature of psychic dreaming, the answers to those questions will remain hidden.

room attempted to telepathically transmit a target image to them. The subjects were then awakened and asked to describe their dreams. The next day, they were shown several possible targets and asked to rank them in terms of matching the content and emotions of their dreams.

Overall, the correlation of dreamed images to the "sent" target images was significantly above the number that could have occurred by chance.[6] Sometimes volunteers experienced precognition, dreaming of the correct target images a day or two in advance. The rapport between sender and dreamer was an important factor in success.

Researcher Harold Sherman did informal experiments with dream telepathy and telepathic suggestion. He found he obtained the best results with both sending and receiving impressions when in a relaxed state bordering on the hypnagogic stage. Sherman also discovered that he could use the same exercises to harness the tremendous creative power of the subconscious mind. He would visualize what he desired to achieve, such as meeting someone he needed to see. The subconscious mind would attract the elements needed to materialize the goal. He experimented doing these visualizations when he was certain that others would be asleep, and therefore more likely to be receptive to his telepathic images.

He also learned that suggestions cannot force others to do something against their will. Dream telepathy, he said, is not a way to control people.

IDENTIFYING PSYCHIC ELEMENTS IN DREAMS

Most people experience at least one psychic dream in life, and some people have them frequently. How does a person know when a dream is ordinary and when it is psychic? Few dreams of car crashes and airplane accidents are psychic. Rather, they are ordinary dreams using those symbols to give personal messages to the dreamer.

People who have frequent psychic dreams learn over time to recognize the signals, which can be different for each dreamer. For example, many psychic dreams seem exceptionally "real" and not dreamlike. The dreamer may have intense emotions, especially bad feelings if the dream is a precognition of a disaster. There may be certain symbols in a dream that say "psychic" to one dreamer but not necessarily another.

Dreamwork, the interpretation of dreams, including psychic ones, is not an exact science. Ultimately, a person must simply devote time to recording and interpreting dreams in order to gain a broad understanding of them. It is discussed in Chapter 9.

Dreams That Heal

In ancient Greece a man who has been chronically ill is on the most important journey of his life. Agares has been granted permission to make a pilgrimage to Epidaurous, one of the largest healing temples in the known world. Actually, it is a dream-healing temple, for while Agares is there, he will try to dream his healing. No earthly doctor has been able to help him. This is his last hope.

Agares is part of a group of pilgrims who are all seeking dream healing. They take offerings of coins, food, and animals to the temple. They are amazed by Epidaurous. It is like a small city, with numerous buildings. There are houses for the dream priests, dormitories for the pilgrims, baths, and a huge outdoor amphitheater for lectures and entertainment. The pilgrims are shown their tiny cells, where they will sleep on mats and dream.

After a ritual of purification that includes bathing and putting on clean clothing, Agares meets with a dream priest and explains his illness. The priest listens thoughtfully, and then instructs him for dreaming. Agares is to light a certain oil lamp and recite certain prayers asking Asklepios, the god of healing, to come to him in his dreams and heal him.

The rest of the day and evening are spent in prayer. Before he retires, Agares is given an herbal drink to help him sleep deeply. He drinks, makes his final prayer, and then sleeps.

Figure 8.1 *A reproduction of Epidaurous shows the stadium* (left) *and the main temple* (right), *which was dedicated to Askelpios, the Greek god of medicine and healing. Ailing people would discuss their illness with a priest here and then sleep overnight on couches. The next morning the temple priests would interpret their dreams for a cure.* (SSPL/The Image Works)

He dreams that he is visited by a glowing old man carrying a snake-entwined staff, and accompanied by a dog. The old man touches him but does not speak.

The next morning Agares meets with the priest and relates his dream. The priest tells him he has been gifted healing by the touch of the god. He will go home restored. Agares dictates a testimony, which the priest engraves on a lead tablet that will remain at the temple to inspire other pilgrims and give them hope.

Dreams have been valued around the world as a source of healing for thousands of years. In the ancient world, dreams had three primary purposes: to forecast the future, to provide the guidance of the gods, and to aid healing. Records show that all kinds of ailments and conditions were cured with the help of dreams, from chronic illnesses to blindness and lameness.

The dreaming undertaken by Agares is a process called incubation. A dream with a specific purpose is incubated, or birthed, through ritual, request, and prayer. The best place to undertake healing dream incubation was at one of many sacred dream temples scattered throughout the classical world.

Dream healing was practiced in ancient Egypt, too. The greatest temple was at Memphis, near Cairo. It was dedicated to the god of healing, Imhotep, who was a mortal who lived during the Third Dynasty (circa 2980 BCE to 2570 BCE). Imhotep was highly regarded in his time. He was a physician, a skilled architect, and an astrologer to the priests of the sun god, Ra. After death, Imhotep was elevated to the status of god of medicine.

By the first millennium BCE, dream incubation was a widespread practice in Egypt. The Greeks, who borrowed heavily from the Egyptians, also valued dreams, whose healing powers were directed by Asklepios.

Dream healing was absorbed into early Christianity and was given over to angels rather than the pagan gods. Specifically, the archangel Michael took the place of Asklepios and other deities. Michael was petitioned for dream healing by Christian pilgrims to his own sacred sites. The most important of these was a church at Eusebios, near Constantinople. These temples were closed over the centuries as dreams lost their importance in Christianity.

Dreams have been used by other cultures around the world for healing for centuries. The ancient Chinese realized that dreams played an important role in the diagnosis and maintenance of physical health. The understanding of dreams is deeply embedded in Taoism, a system of mysticism and philosophy, and the only native religion of China.

The ancient Chinese compiled and published dream dictionaries and articles, dream diaries, and paintings and woodcuts of dreams in progress. Magical spells against nightmares and bad dreams proliferated. Dream incubation was widely practiced.

Figure 8.2 *A bronze statue shows Imhotep, the Egyptian god of healing, holding an open papyrus scroll.* (Getty Images)

Like others in the ancient world, the Chinese had a dream god, who could be petitioned to grant certain types of dreams. The *Shih-lei t'ung-pien* (Compendium of Literary Allusions) refers to a dream god called *Chih-li*, a name which probably was adopted from foreign sources. *Chih-li* could be invoked for productive dreaming by reciting a mantra or charm seven times before sleep.

DREAM HEALING TODAY

Healing within dreams still occurs today. Instead of being visited by a god, a dreamer might be treated by a modern dream doctor. The images have changed to fit the times, but the purpose of them remains the same. In some healing dreams, people say they are bathed in radiant light that seems not of this world. Or, an angel visits them and touches them. In still other dreams, dreamers are given information via direct messages or in symbols that tell them how to improve healing that is taking place, such as from surgery or an injury.

Medical experts do not know how and why dream healing happens. The ancients believed in visits from the gods during dreams, and so it made sense to them that the gods did the healing. Modern experts think that dreaming may release natural healing powers that exist within the patient.

Still others believe healing dreams to be a combination of inner healing aided by the divine. For reasons we do not understand, these forces seem to be more effective during dreaming sleep than during waking consciousness.

Why doesn't everyone who is sick have a healing dream? No one knows the answer.

DREAMING DIAGNOSES

In addition to aiding healing, dreams also forecast illness before actual symptoms show up in the body. The diagnostic powers of dreams were known to the ancients, including the dream-savvy Greeks.

The famous Greek physician Galen, who lived in the second century BCE, had a dream healing that influenced his medical practice. At age 27 he suffered a potentially fatal condition from an abscess under his diaphragm. He went to a dream temple devoted to Asklepios to dream a cure. He had two dreams in which he opened an artery between the thumb and forefinger and let it bleed until it stopped naturally. He awakened knowing this was the cure. He performed this procedure on himself, which drained his infection, and he was healed.

During the course of his career, Galen performed many operations on his patients based on information obtained from dreams. He said

The Doctor Is In: Astral Travel Walk-ins Welcome

Asklepios was the reigning healer of the ancient dream world. People who were ill would ask him to heal them in their dreams—or at least tell them how they could be healed. Half god, half mortal, Asklepios lived in the dreamy astral world of the gods. To see him required dream astral travel. This was accomplished through ritual and prayer, often at a special, secluded place.

Asklepios could heal because he had been gravely wounded and had healed himself. The dream healer may have been based on a real person by that name—Asklepios means "unceasingly gentle" in Greek—who lived around the eleventh century BCE.

According to myth, Asklepios's mortal mother, Coronis, was unfaithful to her husband, the god Apollo. Outraged, Apollo sent his sister, Artemis, to kill Coronis by shooting her with an arrow. Her body was placed on a funeral pyre. Before the body burned, Apollo snatched the baby Asklepios, fathered by Coronis's lover, from her womb. He gave Asklepios to the centaur Chiron, who raised him in the mountains and taught him the healing arts.

Asklepios became such an excellent healer that he could even raise the dead. This threatened the immortal gods, so Zeus struck him down he had saved many lives as a result. His own experience made him a believer in the diagnostic and healing powers of dreams.

More recently, in the twentieth century, the psychologist Carl G. Jung recognized diagnostic dreams in some of his psychotherapy cases. Like the Greeks, he called them **prodromal dreams**, from the Greek term *prodromos*, or "running before."[1] Jung described cases in which patients had dreams alerting them to life-threatening illnesses before they knew they were sick.

He noted that some patients who dreamed of destruction or injury to horses—an archetypal symbol of the human body—later were

with a thunderbolt and killed him. Zeus placed him in the sky, where he became the constellation Orion.

In the dream world, Asklepios became even more popular and powerful as a healer. At the peak of his cult, about 400 dream temples were built to him. He was also worshiped in sacred groves and caves. He held his office hours at night, seeing patients who journeyed to him through the pathways of the dream world.

How did a person know for certain he met Asklepios in his dreams? The healer had a specific appearance. He looked like an old man with a beard, carrying a staff entwined by a single snake. He was sometimes accompanied by a dog or by a boy dwarf named Telesphorus. The snake symbolized regeneration, wisdom, and healing. The dog symbolized death and rebirth. The dwarf symbolized fertility.

The best healing occurred if a person was touched by Asklepios in a dream. Next best was a prescription: instructions for healing. Sometimes the instructions had to be interpreted by dream priests. Testimonies about miraculous dream healings were recorded at many of the god's temples.

Asklepios still appears in dreams today. Sometimes people do not recognize who he is. Sometimes people in need of healing dream of an old man with a snake-entwined staff and a dog: Asklepios, still on the job in the astral realm.

shown to be in the early stages of serious illness, such as cancer. In at least one case he documented, the illness was caught early enough to be treated successfully.

In his book *Healing Dreams*, author Marc Ian Barasch tells how his cancer of the thyroid was first revealed in disturbing and bizarre dreams. In the dreams, he was chased by an axe murderer trying to decapitate him and was stared at by the figure of Death. A number of his dreams had a neck theme: primitive tribesmen stuck long needles into his "neck-brain"; a World War II bullet was lodged in his neck and removed by a Chinese surgeon; and he found himself crawling about a Mayan "necropolis," a temple to the dead.

These and other dreams caused Barasch to seek medical help earlier than he might have otherwise, possibly saving his life. The doctor at first was skeptical about the dreams and reluctantly ordered tests. The tests revealed early stages of cancer in the thyroid gland (also called the "neck brain"), which is near the larynx.[2]

Diagnosis by dreams is valued in traditional Chinese medicine, which holds that all dreams, pleasant and unpleasant, are produced by imbalances in the body. Thus, by understanding the images and symbols in dreams, one could know the state of one's physical and mental health and gain understanding on remedies for correcting the imbalances. For example, deficiencies in the vital organs produce specific dream images, such as a depleted heart produces dreams of flames, hills, and mountains, while depleted lungs yields dreams of flying and things made of gold and iron.

Unlike traditional Western medicine, which separates mind and body, Chinese medicine makes no clear distinction between the two.

PAYING ATTENTION

Dreams heal more than physical ailments—they also heal emotional wounds. People who are devastated by serious loss often find powerful healing help in their dreams. For example, the following dream helped a 37-year-old woman gain control over severe emotional turmoil in her life. Her father had died, she was experiencing profound grief, and her marriage was in trouble. She felt as though she was losing her sanity, and that she should give up on everything. Then one night she had a dream that helped her recover enough balance to weather the emotional upheaval:

> As I fell asleep, I heard several musical voices calling my name, and I felt a sensation of floating in complete comfort. I saw a beautiful star field, and then a strand of stars separated from the rest, coming toward me. I felt many hands place this beautiful necklace around my neck in a gesture of blessing. I felt a profound sense of love, encouragement and acceptance. I slept well through the night and had the best rest I'd had for many weeks. The depression was gone the next morning and with it the fear and anticipation of panic/anxiety attacks: I have not had one since that night.
>
> Everything in my life did not become "perfect" overnight, but I have regained my self-esteem, and a sense of real security and peace. I often think about that dream, and feel certain that I am loved and cherished by the Creator of that necklace. I know I am wearing it even now—a billion carats worth of stars.[3]

Deriving emotional benefit from a dream is different for every person, depending on the personal meanings associated with the symbols in the dream, the emotional state of the dreamer in waking life and in the dream, and the personal interpretation given to the dream.

Understanding Your Dreams

Amy has the following dream one night:

I have to get new clothes for a special occasion—a party or something. I'm in a store going through racks of cool things. A strange woman comes up to me. She is dressed in very old clothes, like something out of grandma's closet. She looks very out of place. She holds out a dress for me. It looks like an old style like hers. I don't want to take it, but I don't want to offend her, either.

How can Amy make sense out of this dream? Like most dreams, it does not portray something logical. No wonder many people ignore their dreams! But the key to understanding dreams is to *not* look at them as logical, real-life scenarios. Dreams speak in symbols about situations in life and our emotions.

Clothing in dreams is often a symbol of how people want others to think of them.[1] People wear certain styles and outfits to send messages to others about who they are or who they are trying to be. Getting new clothes in a dream can symbolize entering a new phase in life, such as moving to a new town, starting a new school, or getting a new job.

Old clothing can represent the past. Amy did her dream interpretation work and concluded that the new clothing represented a major change in her life. The old woman with old clothing represented a part of her that did not want to let go of the past. The dream helped Amy feel more comfortable about the changes happening in her life. She wanted to keep moving forward and not look back.

The meanings of dreams are seldom obvious. It takes time to understand them. Dreams are like invisible ink. By holding them up to the right light, it is possible to see their meaning clearly.

A dream seldom has only one message. Because symbols are best understood by intuition, they can be read in different ways, and each way can have meaning for the dreamer. A dream is likely to have a primary message, but also to have one or more secondary messages as well. The messages may all relate to the same situation, or they may address multiple things going on in someone's life.

Dreams are highly emotional. They give feedback on how the dreamer is emotionally dealing with life situations. Dreams especially reveal fears and anxieties, which is why so many of them seem negative. Working with dreams gives people insight into how they can deal with stresses, obstacles, setbacks, and so on. Dreaming, even about negative situations and feelings, is beneficial, because it provides insight into how to restore balance in life. Doesn't everyone want to know how to be happier and more fulfilled? Dreamwork helps people find the answers and the ways.

To interpret dreams it is necessary to understand what some of the major symbols often mean, how to interpret them, and how to improve recall of dreams. There is no right or wrong interpretation of dreams; they can have different meanings to people. Carl G. Jung observed that dreams are part of nature and do not deceive, but express something as best they can, just as all things in nature strive to live and prosper as best they can.[2]

There is one rule, however. Dreamwork has changed significantly since ancient times, when people looked to dream priests and specialists to interpret their dreams for them. Today, the emphasis is on the individual. The view held in psychology is that only the dreamer can truly interpret a dream. Others can only help by offering suggestions.

The same applies to dream dictionaries and dream wikis on the Internet. Many symbols in dreams have general meanings that can apply to many people. A dream will always be colored by the dreamer's life, unique situations, personal beliefs, and so on. Thus, even general symbols may have to be modified. Dream dictionaries are excellent starting points for getting ideas. However, they should not be used as the only and final word.

A DREAMWORK PLAN

Understanding dreams gets easier the more someone works with them. Dreams seem to be responsive to a sincere intent. Make a commitment to write down as many dreams as you can in a journal. Dreams are easy to forget, so it's important to record them as soon as possible after waking up. Plan to get up a little earlier than usual to allow enough time for this.

Make a note of the ideas that come concerning the meaning of the dream. Don't try to figure out what's "right." Once the dream is written down, it's possible to go back to it at any time and work on the meaning of it.

Also, don't throw away dreams that feature something done during the previous day or days. Dreams often make use of things fresh in one's mind as ways of creating messages. These are called "day residues." For example, someone goes to see a movie, and that night the person's dream involves the movie in some way. The person is not just rehashing the movie. There is still a message in the dream.

Here are some tips for starting interpretation dreamwork:

1   Give the dream a title. This will help to find the center of the dream.

2   Identify the major symbols: house, fire, people, activity, etc.

3   Make associations with those symbols: "The house reminds me of. . . ."

4   Relate the dream to something going on in your life: "I get lost in the dream, and I feel lost about . . ."

5   Look for simple meanings first. Most dreams are about the dreamer and his or her emotions.

6 Look for puns, slang, and plays on words. Dreams make ample use of all of these. For example, a deer might represent something "dear."

7 Draw the dream.

Play around with words and associations. It should be clear when something hits the target. For example, here is a dream in which the dreamer is driving along narrow winding roads high up on a cliff:

> *I am driving in an automobile down a steep hill and have to pass another car which is on my right, with a steep precipice on my left. I just manage to get by. Then I have to go down to a bridge with a sharp right turn beyond it and have a great fear of meeting another car.*

Driving up and down hills is a common dream drama. Hills often represent challenges, difficulties, and obstacles. The emotional key for the dreamer was the phrase "I just manage to get by." They described how he felt on his job. The dream made him realize that he was under great stress at work and needed to do something about it.

By collecting dreams it will become possible to notice patterns in them. The same symbols and themes may reappear but in slightly different ways. Perhaps these dreams are repeatedly nudging the dreamer about something. Some dreams repeat in nearly the same detail. These often have to do with unresolved issues. It may take an expert's help in working with them.

MAJOR SYMBOLS

Here are some symbols that appear in many dreams and what they can often mean. These meanings do not precisely fit every dream.

○ **Air:** Mental activity, planning, communication.

○ **Animals:** Instinct, impulses, primitive feelings, and physical matters relating to the body. Animals are true to themselves, and often

Figure 9.1 *Recording dreams in a diary is a good way to gain insight into their true meaning.* (Will & Deni McIntyre/ Photo Researchers, Inc.)

10 Most Common Dream Themes

Most dreams deal with anxieties and fears. People worry about their ability to perform in school and on the job, whether or not they are well liked and popular, their self-esteem, where they are going in life, and how they are able to influence and control what happens to them. Dreams also help people address old emotional wounds and face problems.

The following are 10 of the most common dream themes shared by people. Every dream is unique to the dreamer, having personal meanings; however, general meanings common to these dreams may also apply.

1 *Flying.* A release of creative energy. Or, a desire or the ability to escape something unpleasant.

2 *Falling.* Something the dreamer feels is beyond their control.

3 *Losing teeth.* Loss of personal power and control.

4 *Being nude or partially nude in public.* Worry over being "exposed" about your true self, or something you've done.

5 *Being pursued or attacked by a monster or threatening person.* Avoiding a threatening situation in waking life. Or, needing to confront a problem.

6 *Being late.* Avoiding getting something done.

7 *Getting lost.* Not having a clear sense of direction; worry over a choice of action.

8 *Losing money, wallets, purses, and valuables.* Loss of self-confidence or self-esteem.

9 *Being unprepared for a test or examination.* Feeling inadequate concerning something in waking life.

10 *Missing a train, plane, or boat.* Lack of organization and ability to be on top of a situation.

represent traits people associate with them. For example, foxes are clever and shy, bears are protective and fierce, dogs are loyal, cats are independent, and so on.

○ **Automobiles:** The dreamer and how he or she is getting around in life. The model, color, and condition of a dream car can say a lot about the dreamer.

○ **Babies:** A rebirth, a new beginning, something that needs care and attention.

○ **Battles and wars:** Inner conflict, such as in trying to make a difficult decision. Also, conflict going on around the dreamer.

○ **Bridges:** Making a transition or change in life. Bridges relate to relationships and moves, and to all situations in which the dreamer feels a need to change.

○ **Children:** Innocence, playfulness, simplicity, and purity. Depending on the dream, children can symbolize carefree happiness or untroubled times.

○ **Clocks:** Deadlines, running out of time.

○ **Crossroads and intersections:** Choices.

○ **Dancing:** Connecting to the emotions or needing to do so. Dancing well might represent freedom and creative ability. Dancing poorly might mean something crucial in life is out of whack.

○ **Disasters:** Challenges, upsets, and problems, especially major ones that threaten the stability of life.

○ **Doctors, nurses, and health care officials:** The need to have something healed, even on an emotional level. Also, the process of being healed.

○ **Doors:** Opportunities, openings, or barriers. Doors hide things such as secrets. Open doors might symbolize opportunities or invitations to explore something.

○ **Earth:** Physical health, being grounded and stable, personal resources such as energy, health, and money.

- **Earthquake:** An inner shake-up.
- **Eating and food:** Spiritual and emotional nourishment. Overeating in a dream might represent a hunger to satisfy emotional needs.
- **Explosions:** A situation that has gone out of control.
- **Famous people:** Qualities we admire and would like to see in ourselves.
- **Father:** Authority, discipline, rules, logical thinking.
- **Fire:** Destruction, but often with a healing element. Think of how a forest regrows after a major fire. Also, energy and ambition.
- **Fishing:** Searching for something, especially of emotional importance.
- **Forest:** The unknown and mysterious.
- **Grandparents:** Nurturing, caretaking, guardianship. Also, wisdom, knowledge, and things related to the past.
- **Hills:** Obstacles. Also, the way to achieve goals.
- **Home:** Security, safety.
- **Ice:** Frozen emotions.
- **Intruders:** Something or someone who invades privacy or security.
- **Medicine:** A need for healing or the process of being healed.
- **Military:** Enforcers of law and order; protection.
- **Mirrors:** Self-knowledge. Also, the bare truth about something.
- **Money:** A person's value and worth in terms of qualities.
- **Monsters:** Terrors and problems that need to be confronted.
- **Mother:** Nurturing, protection, emotional connection.
- **Mountains:** Challenges.
- **Operations:** Taking care of one's health, emotional or physical, by correcting a problem or getting rid of something.
- **Police:** Inner authority figure who makes certain the rules are followed.

- **Prison:** Limited opportunities, lack of freedom.
- **Telephone:** Communication with the inner self.
- **Trees:** Connections to family, nature, and to different levels of consciousness.
- **Tunnels:** Inner processing.
- **Volcanoes:** Bottled up anger.
- **Water:** Emotions, intuition.

EXAMPLE OF A DREAM INTERPRETATION

Here's how one dreamer interpreted this dream.

> *I am in prison, feeling hopeless. Long corridors stretch out like underground tunnels. Then it becomes a prisoner of war camp. The soldiers are listless and depressed. There are lots of browns, greens, and grays, especially in their uniforms. I suddenly notice that their heads are all cabbages. It becomes a field of cabbages.*

He entitled the dream "Cabbages in Jail." The major symbols that impressed him were prison, tunnels, prisoners of war, and cabbages. He noted the emotional tone of the dream: depression, hopelessness, and dull colors. He associated prison with feeling confined in his life by circumstances beyond his control, the dull prisoners around him and dull colors he associated with his feelings of boredom. Even the cabbages represented dullness to him, because cabbages do not have much flavor. Everywhere he looks is boredom.

The dreamer felt the dream related to his job. It paid well but was not challenging. He had gone into debt and felt he was chained to the job in order to keep up his payments. He realized he had allowed himself to be imprisoned, and that if he really wanted to change, he could manage his debt and find another job. The dream helped him to make a decision to take action rather than allow himself to be a victim.

Figure 9.2 *This collage depicts some of the images and emotions common in nightmares.* (Oscar Burriel/Photo Researchers, Inc.)

WHAT ABOUT NIGHTMARES?

A nightmare is any dream that is troubling to the dreamer. That might be an anxiety dream, like not being prepared for a test, or a more violent dream in which the dreamer is pursued by an attacker. The term "nightmare" comes from the Anglo-Saxon terms *nicht* (night) and *mara* ("the crusher"). In earlier times people believed that outside forces, such as spirits, demons, witches and sorcerers, caused people to have bad dreams, especially by sitting on their chests with crushing force. Sometimes bad dreams were blamed on food.

Today a nightmare is viewed as a symptom of a problem that needs addressing. Stressful dreams that repeat might indicate a situation that the dreamer is trying to ignore, such as a problem in a relationship. Sometimes nightmares are related to deeper problems, such as severe psychological shocks, or even physical illness. Nightmares that are deeply disturbing should be discussed with a professional in medicine or psychology.

Dream It, Do It

Elias Howe is a Massachusetts textile expert, mechanic, and inventor. The year is 1846, and Howe has been working hard to perfect a machine that he knows will revolutionize industry: a sewing machine. There is only one major problem he cannot solve: how to work the thread with the needle.

Howe wonders whether or not to abandon his idea. Then one night he has a vivid and odd dream. He is in a jungle. The natives capture him and threaten to kill him if he can't solve his sewing machine problem. He notices that their spears have holes in the tips.

Howe awakens in great excitement. He has the answer to his problem: put a hole in the needle and put the thread through it. The sewing machine is born, enabling clothing to be mass-produced at cheaper costs.

Howe is but one of a long list of inventors, artists, scientists, philosophers, architects, military commanders, and others who have had astonishing creative breakthroughs in dreams. Many of humankind's greatest advancements and artistic creations have been fueled by nighttime visions. In fact, there is no subject or problem beyond the scope of what dreams can influence.

In ancient times inspirational dreams were believed to be given to humans by the gods. Sometimes the dreams would be in response to situations, and other times instructions came out of the blue.

The Greek philosopher Socrates, while he was in prison awaiting execution, had a recurring dream in which the same dream figure urged him to "set to work and make music." The expression in Greek could refer to any creative art, but Socrates had definite ideas about his interpretation of it. He believed that he had been "making music" for years through his philosophy. He also believed that the dream was urging him to expand his creativity by writing poetry. During his final days, Socrates put Aesop's fables to verse. "God has ordered me to do this, both through oracles and dreams and in all the other ways used by divine providence for giving its commands," he stated.

Numerous examples in Greek literature show that people paid careful attention to instructional dreams and acted upon them. They often commemorated their dreams with a plaque, statue, or chapel, just as Thutmose IV did in ancient Egypt.

Today people still have inspirational dreams. The ideas and instructions in them can come from the dreamer, an authority figure, or even an animal. Sometimes there is no specific authority figure, but the dream has a clear message of instruction.

Here are some of the amazing influences dreams have had on history, science, and culture.

MUSIC

Numerous composers, including Richard Wagner and Beethoven, dreamed some of their classical masterpieces. Mozart often woke up with entire compositions in his head, as though his dreams had organized everything while he slept. When he wrote the compositions down, they needed little revision.

More recently rock music has had dream influences as well. In 1965 Paul McCartney heard the melody for his famous Beatles song "Yesterday" in a dream. The dream was so vivid and the music seemed so familiar to him that first he had to convince himself that he did not dream someone else's music that he had heard and forgotten.

When rock musician Sting left his band, The Police, to embark on a solo career, he had a dream that literally shaped his first solo album. Sting had long acknowledged his use of dreams for song material. For his solo debut, he wished to strike out in a new direction, always risky for a successful artist whose fans usually want more of the same. Sting dreamed of being home in Hampshire, England, looking out over a walled and neat garden. Suddenly a group of rowdy and drunk blue turtles appeared through a hole in the wall and began doing acrobatics, tearing up the garden.

Upon reflecting on the dream, Sting saw the blue turtles as symbols of the subconscious and unrealized potential. Their destruction of the neat and manicured garden represented his desire to destroy preconceptions and expectations about his artistry. As a result, he reached deep within himself to produce the material for his debut album, titled, appropriately, *The Dream of the Blue Turtles*. Several songs became hit singles and the album sold more than three million copies.

ART

Artist and poet William Blake found dreams to be a continuing source of inspiration, as did Salvador Dali and other surrealist artists. Dali received so many ideas for his paintings from hypnagogic dreaming that he developed what he called the "slumber with key" technique and taught it to his students. The technique calls for placing a plate upside down in front of a comfortable armchair, and then settling into the chair for a nap while holding a heavy key between thumb and forefinger, poised over the plate. As one falls deeper into sleep, the key is released and hits the plate, causing awakening. This, said Dali, enables one to capture the dream before it is lost in deeper sleep.[1]

The artist Jasper Johns created many paintings that were unremarkable, until 1954, when he dreamed of himself painting a large American flag. He painted the flag he saw in his dream, entitling it *Flag*. Afterward he became a sensation.

Figure 10.1 *Salvador Dali received artistic inspiration for surrealistic images like this one,* Persistence of Memory, *from hypnagogic dreams, or abstract images that appear between consciousness and sleep.* (Topham/The Image Works)

LITERATURE

Perhaps the most famous dream-inspired fiction is *Frankenstein*, written by Mary Wollstonecraft Shelley, the wife of poet Percy Bysshe Shelley. In 1816 the couple were guests, along with physician and writer John Polidori, of poet Lord Byron at his Swiss chalet. One rainy night, they entertained each other by telling ghosts stories. Byron challenged everyone to write a horror story. That night Mary had a dream about a scientist who brought an artificial man to life.

The idea for the horror novel *Dr. Jekyll and Mr. Hyde* came to author Robert Louis Stevenson in a dream. At the time Stevenson was out of money and was desperate to sell a new work. For two days he had racked his brain for plot ideas, only to come up dry. On the second night he had a dream about a man, pursued for a crime, who took a powder to transform himself. Stevenson said later that would often converse with "little people," or brownies—a type of house fairy—when he was in a borderline state of sleep. They gave him so many ideas that he said he should question who was the real storyteller: him or them.

Horror author Stephen King gets many plot ideas from his dreams. He says that he uses dreams the way a person uses mirrors to see things that cannot be seen directly ahead. His dreams have enabled him to create a string of best-selling novels that have kept readers page-turning in suspense. Some of King's dreams waited years to find their way into his books. A childhood nightmare of a hanged man who came horribly to life and grabbed at King became the inspiration many years later for his vampire novel *'Salem's Lot*.

FILM AND TELEVISION

Some filmmakers have lifted their dreams exactly as they had them into dream scenes in their films. Ingmar Bergman put his dream of four women in mourning in *Cries and Whispers* and a coffin dream in *Wild Strawberries*. Robert Altman's *Three Women* was a story as he dreamed it, though it was not filmed as a dream.

Dan Curtis, a television producer, got the idea for his smash television soap opera, *Dark Shadows*, from a dream in 1965. In the dream he saw a young girl traveling on a train to a brooding mansion in New England. The dream was dark and edgy, with a sense of danger. It left a strong impression on Curtis, and soon he conceived of the wealthy but troubled Collins family, who lived in their mansion, Collinwood, and had a vampire relative named Barnabas Collins.

SCIENCE

In the late 1880s the chemist Friedrich A. Kekulé von Stradonitz made a revolutionary contribution to organic chemistry because of a dream. Kekulé had attempted without success to discover the structure of the benzene molecule. One night he had a dream in which atoms formed long snakelike chains. One snake grabbed its own tail and began to rotate. From this, Kekulé was able to create a model of a closed molecular ring. The symbol of the snake biting its own tail was unknown to him, but it is one of the most important symbols in Western alchemy. It is called the *ouroboros*, and it represents the unity of opposites, wholeness, oneness, and eternity.

USING DREAMS FOR GUIDANCE AND CREATIVITY

In many of the cases above, breakthrough dreams came in a stage of the creative process where the dreamer was stumped for ideas about

How to Ask Your Dreams for Ideas and Answers

Dreams are an excellent way to access your intuition and get answers to questions that are in your best interests. Dreams sort through what you think you want versus what is best. Here is a simple process for asking your dreams for advice.

1 Choose an important matter and be open-minded about the answer.

2 Phrase a short, simple question you would like your dreams to answer. For example:

- Should I (proposed action)
- How can I solve (problem)
- How can I improve my relationship with (name)
- Give me an idea for (project)
- Show me my path

how to move forward or solve a problem. It seems as though the waking mind had to get out of the way for the answer to be recognized.

People who pay attention to their dreams learn how to ask dreams for specific information rather than wait for inspired lightning to strike. While they sleep, their dreams mine rich fields of ideas. Sometimes the ideas are presented in dreams, and sometimes they are simply "known" to the dreamer upon awakening, or later in the day.

Inspired dreams speak in symbols just as ordinary dreams do. This is why it is important to do regular work with dreams to gain a good understanding of their language.

Take the case of an Indian dream psychologist, Anjali Hazarika, who conducted dream creativity workshops for petroleum engineers. A chemist in one of his groups was seeking to develop enzymes that

3   Write the question in your dream journal.

4   Think about the question throughout the day.

5   At bedtime, write the question again, and instruct yourself to have and remember a dream that will answer the question.

6   Upon awakening, record whatever you have dreamed, even if it does not seem to answer the question.

7   Give extra attention to dream interpretation. Look for answers hidden in symbols.

8   Watch for more information that pops into your mind later.

9   If the answer still is not clear, try the process again. Try rephrasing the question.

Practice makes perfect with this process, so don't give up too easily. If a while goes by and you feel your question remains unanswered, ask yourself if you are trying to get an answer you want, rather than what your dreams are really trying to tell you.

would refine crude oil. Finally at a loss for ideas, he asked his dreams for help. He dreamed of standing on the side of a road while a big truck full of rotting cabbages went past. The stink was tremendous. At first, neither the chemist nor any of his associates could make sense of the dream. A few days later, the chemist was working in his laboratory when he realized that the bacteria produced by rotting cabbages broke down into the very enzymes he needed. What was more, cabbages were exceptionally cheap.

EXPLORE YOUR DREAMSCAPE

Over the course of time you will spend an average of one-third of your entire life asleep. That adds up to quite a few years, some of which will be spent dreaming. Make the most of your dream time by learning to understand the valuable messages your dreams give you. Take advantage of the opportunities dreams provide to enrich and improve your life. Dreams never lose their excitement and mystery. Enjoy your adventures!

Timeline

1400s BCE Prince Thutmose of Egypt is told in a dream how he can become pharaoh

356 Alexander the Great is born, supposedly the result of dream magic

44 Calpurnia, wife of Julius Caesar, dreams of his assassination the night before it happens on March 15

415 CE St. Augustine writes the oldest known Western account of lucid dreams

1200s-1800s Dreams decline in importance in the West

1743 Emanuel Swedenborg begins his astral travels to the afterlife

1816 Mary Wollstonecraft Shelley has a dream that results in one of the greatest horror novels, *Frankenstein*

1846 Elias Howe invents the sewing machine from a dream

1865 In early April President Abraham Lincoln dreams of his death and within two weeks is assassinated

1880s Psychical researchers begin studying the paranormal aspects of dreams

1899 Anthropologists coin the term "Dreamtime" to describe Aboriginal concepts of dreams versus waking reality

1900 Sigmund Freud's *The Interpretation of Dreams* is published

1902–1938 Oliver Fox records his astral travel dream experiences

1914 On June 27 Bishop Joseph Lanyi has a precognitive dream about the assassination of Yugoslavia's Archduke Ferdinand and his wife the following day, triggering the start of World War I

1915–1950 Sylvan Muldoon researches astral travel dreams

1917   The *Titantic* sinks on April 12, but some people avoid the disaster thanks to their precognitive dreams

1953   Scientists link dreaming to rapid eye movement (REM) stages of sleep

1958   Robert A. Monroe has his first astral travel dreams

1960s   Dream telepathy research conducted at Maimonides Medical Center in Brooklyn, New York

1965   Paul McCartney dreams the Beatles' hit "Yesterday"

1966   The October 26 coal slide in Aberfan, Wales, was previewed in precognitive dreams

1967   British Premonitions Bureau is established in London to collect early warnings in precognitive dreams

1968   Central Premonitions Bureau is established in New York to complement the British Premonitions Bureau

1970s   Scientific research of lucid dreams increases

1980s   Premonitions bureaus close due to lack of success

2001   The September 11 terrorist attacks on the World Trade Center and Pentagon are seen in advance in numerous precognitive dreams

Glossary

ARCHETYPE A symbol with cosmic or mythic significance that can appear in a dream

ASTRAL BODY A double of the physical body that serves as a vehicle in astral travel dreaming

ASTRAL CORD An umbilical cord that connects the physical body to the astral body, sometimes seen in astral travel dreams

ASTRAL PLANE A shadowy realm that duplicates the physical world, where some dreaming takes place

ASTRAL TRAVEL Traveling out-of-body to distant locations while dreaming

EXCEPTIONAL HUMAN EXPERIENCE An experience often involving a spiritual component that deeply affects a person

HYPNAGOGIC Occurring during a stage of falling asleep between wakefulness and sleep, often filled with jumbled dream images and sounds

HYPNAPOMPIC STATE A stage of awakening between sleep and wakefulness, often filled with jumbled dream images and sounds

INCUBATION A process of mental suggestion, sometimes combined with ritual, to have a specific dream

LUCID DREAMING/LUCIDITY The awareness of dreaming while dreaming, with varying degrees of control over a dream

MUTUAL DREAMING Two or more persons sharing the same dream, or similar contents of a dream

PRECOGNITIVE DREAMING/PRECOGNITION Dreaming a future event

PREMONITION A vague feeling about a future event, usually negative

PRODROMAL DREAMS   Dreams that forecast illness before symptoms manifest

RAPID EYE MOVEMENT **(REM)**   A stage of sleep characterized by fluttering eyelids and other physiological signs that is accompanied by dreaming

TELEPATHIC DREAMING   The ability to send and receive messages or dreams with another person; the recipient is asleep

TELEPATHY   The transmission of thoughts from one person to another

Endnotes

CHAPTER 1

1. Monford Harris, *Studies in Jewish Dream Interpretation* (Northvale, NJ: Jason Aronson, Inc., 1994), 50.

2. Patricia Cox Miller, *Dreams in Late Antiquity: Studies in the Imagination of a Culture* (Princeton: Princeton University Press, 1994), 17.

3. Steven M. Oberhelman, ed., *The Oneiricriticon of Achmet: A Medieval and Arabic Treatise on the Interpretation of Dreams* (Lubbock, Tex.: Texas Tech University, 1991), 30–31.

CHAPTER 2

1. Morton Kelsey, *God, Dreams and Revelation: A Christian Interpretation of Dreams* (Minneapolis: Augsburg Publishing House, 1991), 136–137.

2. Ibid., 156.

3. Rosemary Ellen Guiley, *Harper's Encyclopedia of Mystical and Paranormal Experience* (San Francisco: HarperSanFrancisco, 1991), 161.

4. Sigmund Freud, *The Interpretation of Dreams* (New York: The Modern Library, 1950), 120.

5. Carl G. Jung, *Memories, Dreams, Reflections* (New York: Vintage Books, 1965), 306.

CHAPTER 3

1. Robert L. Van de Castle, *Our Dreaming Mind* (New York: Ballantine Books, 1994), 231–235.

2. Montague Ullman, "Dreams as Exceptional Human Experiences," *ASPR Newsletter* XVIII, no. 4, (1995): 6.

CHAPTER 4

1. Stephen LaBerge, *Lucid Dreaming* (New York: Ballantine Books, 1985), 21–22.

2. Jayne Gackenbach and Jane Bosveld, *Control Your Dreams* (New York: Harper & Row, 1989), 16.

3. LaBerge, 80.

CHAPTER 5

1. Oliver Fox, *Astral Projection: A Record of Out-of-the-Body Experiences* (Secaucus, NJ: The Citadel Press, 1962), 34.

2. Robert Crookall, *Out-of-the-Body Experiences: A Fourth Analysis* (New York: University Books, 1970), 69.

3. Linda Lane Magallon, *Mutual Dreaming* (New York: Pocket Books, 1997), 98.

CHAPTER 6

1. Robert Monroe, *The Ultimate Journey* (New York: Doubleday, 1994), 5–6.

2. Michael Talbot, *The Holographic Universe* (New York: HarperCollins, 1991), 272–273.

CHAPTER 7

1. Guiley, *Harper's Encyclopedia of Mystical and Paranormal Experience*, 162.

2. Ian Stevenson, "Seven More Paranormal Experiences Associated with the Sinking of the Titanic," *Journal of the American Society for Psychical Research* 59 (1965): 211–224.

3. W.E. Cox, "Precognition: An Analysis, II," *Journal of the American Society for Psychical Research* 50, no. 1 (January 1956): 99–109.

4. Rosemary Ellen Guiley, *The Dreamer's Way: Using Proactive Dreaming for Creativity and Healing* (New York: Berkley, 2004), 120–121.

5. Ibid., 124–125.

6. Montague Ullman and Stanley Krippner with Alan Vaughan, *Dream Telepathy: Experiments in Nocturnal ESP* (Baltimore: Penguin, 1973), 271–279.

CHAPTER 8

1. Patricia Garfield, *The Healing Power of Dreams* (New York: Simon & Schuster, 1991), 60–61.

2. Marc Ian Barasch, *Healing Dreams: Exploring Dreams That Can Transform Your Life* (New York: Riverhead Books, 2000), 2–3.

3. Guiley, *The Dreamer's Way*, 89–90.

CHAPTER 9

1. Jean Dalby Clift and Wallace B. Clift, *Symbols of Transformation in Dreams* (New York: Crossroad, 1989), 57–58.

2. Jung, 161–162.

CHAPTER 10

1. Guiley, *The Dreamer's Way*, 58.

Bibliography

Barasch, Marc Ian. *Healing Dreams: Exploring Dreams That Can Transform Your Life.* New York: Riverhead Books, 2000.

Barrett, Deirdre. *The Committee of Sleep: How Artists, Scientists, and Athletes Use Dreams for Creative Problem-Solving—and How You Can Too.* New York: Crown, 2001.

Brown, Rustie. *The Titanic the Psychic and the Sea.* Lomita, Calif.: Blue Harbor Press, 1981.

Crookall, Robert. *Out-of-the-Body Experiences: A Fourth Analysis.* New York: University Books, 1970.

Fox, Oliver. *Astral Projection: A Record of Out-of-the-Body Experiences.* Secaucus, N.J.: The Citadel Press, 1962.

Gackenbach, Jayne and Jane Bosveld. *Control Your Dreams.* New York: Harper & Row, 1989.

Garfield, Patricia. *Creative Dreaming.* New York: Fireside, 1995.

——— . *The Healing Power of Dreams.* New York: Simon & Schuster, 1992.

Green, Celia and Charles McCreery. *Lucid Dreaming: The Paradox of Consciousness During Sleep.* London: Routledge, 1994.

Guiley, Rosemary Ellen. *Dreamspeak: How to Understand the Messages in Your Dreams.* New York: Berkley Books, 2001.

——— . *Dreamwork for the Soul: A Spiritual Guide to Dream Interpretation.* New York: Berkley Books, 1998.

——— . *The Dreamer's Way.* New York: Berkley Books, 2004.

LaBerge, Stephen. *Lucid Dreaming.* New York: Ballantine Books, 1985.

LaBerge, Stephen and Howard Rheingold. *Exploring the World of Lucid Dreaming.* New York: Ballantine Books, 1990.

Kirven, Robert H. *Angels in Action: What Swedenborg Saw and Heard*. West Chester, Pa.: Chrysalis Books, 1994.

Magallon, Linda Lane. *Mutual Dreaming*. New York: Pocket Books, 1997.

Monroe, Robert A. *Far Journeys*. Garden City, N.Y.: Dolphin/Doubleday, 1985.

——. *Journeys Out of the Body*. Garden City, N.Y.: Broadway Books, 1991.

——. *Ultimate Journey*. New York: Doubleday, 1994.

Muldoon, Sylvan and Hereward Carrington. *The Projection of the Astral Body*. Whitefish, Mont: Kessinger Publishing, 2003.

Rhine, Louisa. *ESP in Life and Lab: Tracing Hidden Channels*. New York: Collier Books, 1967.

Ullman, Montague and Stanley Krippner with Alan Vaughan. *Dream Telepathy: Experiments in Nocturnal ESP*. Baltimore: Penguin, 1973.

Van de Castle, Robert L. *Our Dreaming Mind*. New York: Ballantine Books, 1995.

Wolf, Fed Alan. *The Dreaming Universe*. New York: Simon & Schuster, 1995.

Further Resources

International Association for the Study of Dreams

http://www.iasdreams.org

A nonprofit, international organization dedicated to the pure and applied investigation of dreams and dreaming. The Web site has information on member benefits, activities, study and discussion groups, events, magazine, professional journal, books, and articles.

Dream Network

http://www.dreamnetwork.net

This Web site has a quarterly magazine of articles and information on dream resources.

The Lucidity Institute, Inc.

http://www.lucidity.com

Organization founded in 1987 by lucid dreaming researcher Dr. Stephen LaBerge to support research on lucid dreams and to help people learn to use them to enhance their lives. The Lucidity Institute's primary mission is to advance research on the nature and potentials of consciousness and to apply the results of this research to the enhancement of human health and well-being. Lucidity Institute members participate in experiments and receive a newsletter.

DREAMS Foundation

http://www.dreams.ca

A Canadian organization founded by Craig Webb that explores dreams and dreaming in conjunction with dream laboratories. The foundation's aims are to inform both the public and health/science professionals about the nature of dreams and their practical applications in relationship to overall health and well-being, and to support research.

European Association for the Study of Dreams
http://www.oniros.fr/home.html
The European Association for the Study of Dreams promotes awareness and appreciation of dreams in the general public as well as within the scientific community. The organization offers activities, events, and resources.

Dream Library
http://www.dreamgate.com/dream/library/idx_organizations.htm
A list of organizations devoted to dreams, dream interpretation, dream study and research, and dream resources.

Index

About the Author and Consulting Editor

ROSEMARY ELLEN GUILEY is one of the foremost authorities on the paranormal. Psychic experiences in childhood led to her lifelong study and research of paranormal mysteries. A journalist by training, she has worked full time in the paranormal since 1983 as an author, presenter, and investigator. She has written 41 nonfiction books on paranormal topics, translated into 14 languages, and hundreds of articles. She has experienced many of the phenomena she has researched. She has appeared on numerous television, documentary, and radio shows. She has appeared in docudramas produced by Spooked TV Productions. She is a columnist for *TAPS Paramagazine*, a consulting editor for *FATE* magazine, and a former writer for the "Paranormal Insider" blog. Ms. Guiley's books include *The Encyclopedia of Angels*, *The Encyclopedia of Magic and Alchemy*, *The Encyclopedia of Saints*, *The Encyclopedia of Vampires, Werewolves, and Other Monsters*, and *The Encyclopedia of Witches, Witchcraft and Wicca*, all from Facts On File. She lives in Maryland and her Web site is http://www.visionaryliving.com.